MIDLAND THI

BY THE SAME AUTHOR

The Houses Behind (Allen & Unwin 1947)

Children Never Tell (Allen & Unwin 1949)

When You Are Old (Allen & Unwin 1951)

The Last Kings of Thule - a translation of the French book by Jean Malaurie (Allen & Unwin 1956)

Between Two Worlds - a book of verse (Outposts 1978)

The Leavises - The first essay (Cambridge University Press)

A Zeppelin in my Childhood (Charles Skilton 1989)

United Family Record (Brewin 1989)

Alma Mater (Girton College 1990)

Scriptural Beasts (Charles Skilton 1991)

World of an Artist (Brewin 1991)

Ways of Loving (Brewin 1993)

The Dodona Oak (Brewin 1995)

Anna with Tristram (Brewin 1996)

Flora at School (Ergon Press 1994)

Cover photograph:
Corporation Street, Birmingham, 1930's.
(Birmingham Post & Mail)

Midland Thirties

Memoirs of a Journalist

Gwendolen Freeman

BREWIN BOOKS

First published in 1998 by

Brewin Books,
Studley,
Warwickshire,
B80 7LG

ISBN 1 85858 061 7

British Library Cataloguing in Publication Data.
A Catalogue record for this book is available from
the British Library

Typeset in Plantin by Avon Dataset, Bidford-on-Avon, Warwickshire, B50 4JH
Printed in Great Britain by Supaprint (Redditch) Limited.

Midlands Thirties

'It reminds me of hell,' I said at New Street Station. 'Dim, dusty, with great voices shouting, milling crowds and rubbish everywhere.'

It was in the seventies, and I had come back to the new city. 'I hope I shall be able to find the way,' said my friend who had driven from Alvechurch to meet me. 'I never come into town now.'

In the old days when I returned to Birmingham after I had left for work in London I had always had the sentimental feeling of coming back to an old home. I had almost shed tears at the sight of a Number Four Harborne bus. I had watched for faces I knew. I had listened with pleasure to the broad Birmingham voices. But now all had changed.

Following that circuitous machine-made course among direction signals, concrete towers and motorways where no one could walk – all giving a feeling of being boxed in and threatened – I felt nothing but a desire to escape. This was not my Birmingham. I recognised nothing.

My friend muttered to herself, trying to find the way out. 'Ah, that's it,' she said at last, and drove a little more quickly. Now we were on the straight Bristol Road that forty years before I had known with trams lurching between trees; and the trees were still there but larger. Gradually, with the concrete towers disappearing behind us, I began faintly to recover the feeling of the old south-western suburbs – leafy Bournville, Kings Norton with neat gardens, the road to the Lickey Hills which were Birmingham's old playground. Of course buildings had crept up everywhere eating the fields, but the bright red brick houses were of human size; and so we went on till we reached Alvechurch, spreading much further but with the old roads still there. Now the towers of central Birmingham were like a bad dream.

I had still after all those years kept the picture of the old Birmingham which I saw for the first time in 1930. I still keep it – the wooden bridge with its tin advertisements for sausages over New Street Station, the old narrow New Street running from the Town Hall and Victorian statues down to the shabby, noisy Bull Ring, with its steep wet streets and stalls and kerb-side sellers. The French-château Post Office, the tall clock, the curious hump of the war

1

memorial were not beautiful, but they were on a human scale, and the streets were for people. The Birmingham that only a few living people have seen is still clear in my mind, and I suppose will continue to stay there.

Birmingham was my home from 1930 for fifteen years. Looking at those years with a historical eye, one sees them as a preparation for the war; a time of mounting crisis leading up to an event that changed the world for ever. But to us it was not at all like that. We did not know – at any rate at the beginning – that we were preparing for anything. We worked, read the local news, had friends and emotional affairs, and went away for holidays just as people had done since the previous war. We tended to look back rather than forward – especially in Birmingham. Proud provincial cities, still largely ignored by London in those pre-television days, boasted of their reforms, products and importance. Birmingham's motto was 'Forward' I was told almost at once; but her pride lay in backward glances – the Chamberlains, the Cadburys and those other manufacturers and charitable city fathers, and further back the clever men who initiated the Industrial Revolution, Boulton and Watt and their Lunar Society.

I came new to this local pride. I arrived, hardly grown up, from the south and from Cambridge and had no idea what an industrial city was like. I did not even know Birmingham's geographical position. We were hazy about the regions in those days of little motoring. But when you work on a local paper, as I was to do, you live in an atmosphere of civic pride. Also, I was interested in history, and soon began to delve into Birmingham's past. Finally I became an enthusiastic daughter of the Midlands and never wanted to return to London.

I must have seen the place, I think now, in a way different from anybody else's.

First Sight

The Daily had a tall corner London office in Fleet Street. I felt like a deceiver when I first stood before it one morning in January.

The last six months had been confusing and mainly boring and unhappy. I had left Cambridge with its charming academic life for a dirty brick building leading from Chancery Lane. I had not wanted to teach and after enquiries had been offered a learning job with a woman's magazine. It had been a glossy weekly for the wealthy – we were always told that it had been read by dowagers in Ireland – but the readership had declined and it had been bought by a member of the Harmsworth family with the aim of making it popular with typists. New staff, except for one indignant secretary, were brought in at low wages, and it was a place of tension and backbiting.

I had never had enough to do at that office and was untrained and academic. The magazine did not prosper as had been hoped, but I was in too humble a position to know much about it. It was better when Bernard, a trained journalist, was brought in to write about furniture and antiques. We shared a room and he lectured me on the craft of journalism – how you could make money as a freelance by cutting out other people's articles and combining their facts. He was very cynical about journalism itself, the office and the people working in it, and he made me feel not quite such a failure. But then came the incident of the borders.

Bernard said it was the editress's fault. I thought so too. She left me to prepare a page of pictures without telling me to follow a new style with the photographs. I marked the page in the old way. It was all wrong and the page had to be re-done at great expense – and the magazine could not afford great expense. The proprietor was angry; the editress had one of her frequent bad headaches, and I found a note on grandiose paper on my desk saying that I was not quite suitable for the post and asking me to leave.

It was one of the unhappiest times of my life. It would have been worse without Bernard. He gave me more instruction on how to write salable articles – but all mine came back – and he looked out for job advertisements. One day he saw an advertisement in *The Times* saying that a woman editor was needed for a Birmingham paper. He gave it to me and told me to apply.

I said that this would be ridiculous. I had had almost no experience and had been a failure; and in any case how could I live in Birmingham? Bernard came from Wolverhampton and said that the Daily was a good paper and it could not do any harm to try. We argued, and I gave in.

The applicant had to send in some of her work. I gathered a few miserable pieces that I had written for the magazine. Bernard suggested that I should put in one of his pieces too – on the grounds that I had been with him when he had visited a shop to write about its furniture. The whole thing seemed a farce, and journalism, according to him, was a profession in which one played tricks; but I would not claim that article as mine. He threw it at me, and I threw it back. Then I posted my application without the slightest expectation of any answer and as far as I remember went back to writing a history of oranges, looked up in the local library, because it was marmalade time. It was to come back like the other articles of those days.

Then, to my astonishment and to Bernard's jubilation, I received a summons to an interview. But of course, I said to him, I could not go to Birmingham, and in any case there was not the faintest chance that I should be asked to.

Geo. W.H.

I did not feel that the Birmingham paper was real till I saw the lady behind the counter. I was to learn later that she was known for her amiable character; but she was not the only one. A benevolent rule creates kindness in the subjects.

I was expected, the lady said in a soft Scottish voice, and she led the way up some steep stairs. The letter summoning me had come from a 'Geo. W.H.', the Birmingham editor, and I had half-consciously noted the smooth handwriting – no typing – and the old-fashioned 'Geo.' It was something different from the dressed-up elbowing characters I had known on the magazine.

The lady opened a door and I saw a spare man with a close-clipped greying beard. In a period when there were few beards he reminded me of a salesman in an old-fashioned draper's shop. The gossip I heard later was that he had grown a beard to hide a weak chin, but his generous level-headed behaviour to me and to others was certainly not weak. But, like many characters of the Daily, he was known as 'shy' and did not chat easily.

Geo. W. was smoking a cigarette with a long holder. Holders were fashionable at the time, and in those days there was no idea that smoking might be bad for you. He chain-smoked and had a perpetual small cough, and he would say in his dry way, 'It's because I smoke too much.' This may have been a result of family troubles – a son whom he never mentioned who had faded away with diabetes, for which in those days little could be done, and a formidable wife. The wife too had died, and he was now married to her sister. They at least got on well, and he probably was as happy now as he had ever been.

But, facing him for the first time, I noticed very little. I expected nothing from the interview and answered his questions only as a matter of form, secretly feeling a cheat. Yet as the interview continued I began to want to make a good impression and pretended that I was seriously considering the job.

Geo. W. was not encouraging. He said that many women, some with long experience, had applied for the post. He thought I was far too young. Did I know anything about the Midlands? I did not. He did, however, to my surprise, ask me about Cambridge. The magazine boss, in that other interview, had told me I must forget Cambridge, as blue stockings were not wanted in journalism. Geo. W. said that the son of his assistant editor was at Cambridge.

He seemed greatly occupied with the important change his paper was about to make. It was going to have a 'women's page' for the first time. At that period staid provincial newspapers were beginning to follow the London press in providing one special page for women. Women had taken over men's jobs in the war. They had the vote. The women's page was a recognition of their greater importance, though it was a strange recognition since it set their interests in a box apart from men's. Later we few women journalists of Birmingham had the feeling that we were considered inferior, doomed to a lower range of interests. But at least women's pages gave us a chance to work on newspapers.

To Geo. W. this step by his solid 'Unionist' paper was a revolutionary development of the utmost importance. He was obviously anxious about it. Up to that time there had been no woman journalist on the Daily in Birmingham. He said, however, that the London office had two 'ladies' engaged on a 'London Letter'. In those days and for long afterwards London was so separate from provincial towns and so much the centre of the country that the large provincial papers had these collections of London diary notes, written in a more personal way than the ordinary news. The Daily had a London Letter and in the usual special-category way a 'London Letter for Women'. The two 'ladies', working from the London office, produced three paragraphs each a day. Their letter would be the first item in the future women's page.

And then we came up against the problem that was always there in this artificial separation of the sexes. What exactly are women's interests? 'Some domestic material, of course,' Geo. W. said. 'And –

er – gardening perhaps. Fashions are dealt with by the London Letter. Some articles perhaps of more general interest . . . I don't myself,' he added with a comical air, 'know what the ladies like.' It was the attitude of the day – that women formed a mysterious kingdom of which men were entirely ignorant.

He asked me how I should procure articles if I got the job. Remembering the way Bernard pored over advertisements, I suggested announcements in *The Times* and the *Daily Telegraph*. Faintly the feeling touched me that there might be some satisfaction in this job after all and that there really was no important reason why I should not go to Birmingham. But Geo. W.'s last words were, 'But I think you're too young.'

I went back to report to Bernard. I repeated Geo. W.'s comment that I was too young. 'You'll get the job,' he said. I said that of course I should not; there were crowds of women after it. I went back to writing articles on 'looked up' subjects.

Three days later I had a note from Geo. W. saying that he was offering me the job.

First Harvest

I arrived at the Daily's Fleet Street office to begin my work on a Monday morning in late January. I was still half thinking that the appointment was a mistake. Geo. W. had offered me the enormous salary of eight pounds a week. I had been earning three with the magazine. My first reaction had been to wonder what I should do with the money.

My anxious family had been relieved that I had found a job. Birmingham in those days was a very long way from the Thames Valley, but I was twenty-one and I had been away at Cambridge, and they had grown used to my absence from home.

Bernard beamed. He had been right after all. In a spirit of revenge after what he considered ill treatment by the magazine editress he had told her that I had been appointed woman editor on *The Times*. 'One for her,' he said. She had, however, produced a surprisingly complimentary reference for me, and I had sent this to Geo. W.

He had asked me to draft advertisements inviting articles, and he would have them inserted. He reckoned that by the following Monday something would have come in, and I was to begin the job by going through what there was. He suggested I should work at the Fleet Street office for three days and on the Thursday move to Birmingham. He would find some accommodation.

The future was a blank. The scar of the months with the magazine remained. I never wanted to work on a London paper again. As a result I was ready to appreciate Birmingham, which few southerners did in those days.

But first I must get to know the London office. Geo. W. had gone, but the sweet-voiced Scottish lady behind the counter received me. 'We have found a small room for you. There is a great deal of post.' So there really was a job.

With daily papers, produced at night, the tempo increases as the day goes on, and at ten in the morning nobody much is about. This office seemed empty as the lady took me upstairs, but I had a shock when she showed me into a room overlooking Fleet Street. A table was completely covered with envelopes of many shapes and sizes, some tied in bundles, some loose. As I sat down a boy brought in another pile. Those advertisements for articles had had their effect.

There had never been enough work for me on the magazine. Here there seemed work for days. A faint glow of relief came over me as I looked down over Fleet Street – not the shabby side street of the magazine but the main thoroughfare with buses jolting by, boys running across the road and groups at corners. Fleet Street was a cheerful place in those days, and the sight of its busy-ness added to the sense of relief. Then I turned to the table.

Geo. W. had left me some 'editor regrets' slips for the return of articles and said that I was to have my own 'woman editor regrets' slips later. I certainly needed those slips. With the economic slump beginning so that more people were trying to earn money with casual writing, with most married women still held at home with time to indulge in scribbling, there must have been thousands of freelance articles going the rounds. There was no television to absorb articles, and there must have been many more magazines and papers on the market. Much of the stuff sent out, of course, like my early efforts, would never find a home. It has always been a wasteful system, this sending out of unsolicited writings – and one fraught with emotion and disappointment. The impression of waste of effort and of trembling emotions assailed me as I opened all those envelopes.

The material was not attractive. Our advertisements had brought in efforts that had been the rounds many times. I opened clean envelopes to find filthy typescripts marked with rusty paper clips, tea-cup bottoms, cigarette scorches, editorial scribbles, grime in the folds. Most of the offerings were wildly unsuitable. The authors seemed to think that anything might do for a page about to be created. Somebody sent a novel 'in case you can use part of it'. There were stories of ten thousand words and verse running to four sheets. There were children's stories about bunnies, which were so much more part of nature and the juvenile world than today, and about fairies who were still flitting round in the non-scientific 'thirties. There were, of course, many household hints of the kind that Bernard had told me to write, but they were very ordinary or so outlandish (culled from recipes of the past) that I could not imagine anyone using them.

Some of the authors seemed in desperate need to confide in somebody. They wrote of family tragedies, loneliness, sickness, children to support. Schoolgirls wrote sending me essays and saying that they always got A. The advertisements had travelled abroad, for people living in Europe – because, they pointed out, they were so poor – offered to supply regular articles on French or Italian cookery. Some weeks later I was to receive enthusiastic offers of help from Australia.

One letter came from a student of my year at Cambridge – a rather withdrawn and not very elegant girl. Writing to 'Dear Madam', she wanted to supply me with fashion articles. One letter frightened me. It simply said, 'If you don't accept this I shall commit suicide.' The manuscript was no good. I could have asked Geo. W. for advice but had not the courage. So I kept the typescript for some weeks, afraid to send it back. Finally I returned it with a sympathetic note. I heard no more; so perhaps the suicide took place.

Many of the would-be correspondents paid themselves compliments. 'I have had my poems published widely in Yorkshire' or 'I have assisted well-known charities with my stories.' But then, I thought, do you not have to praise yourself when you want work published?

Having suffered myself from the flopping back of envelopes on the mat, I felt at first sorry for all these unhappy people. I scribbled sympathetic notes on the rejection slips, but this, I was to find in a few days, was a stupid thing to do. Writers, receiving such sympathy, immediately sent a flood more of unsuitable stuff. It seemed that the verse-writers were the most persistent. When I told them that the paper did not publish verse they still asked to 'fill a corner' or wanted information on papers that did publish poetry.

I ended with a small batch of not impossible articles – travel, a bit of history, something about children. I was afraid that Geo. W. would think me incompetent to have gathered so little and such mediocre writings. But there were so many doubts ahead that one more added little to the burden.

London Staff

I was introduced to what seemed crowds of journalists in my three days at the London office. At that time, with the cities seeming so remote from one another, most provincial papers had their offices along Fleet Street, with quite large staffs writing parliamentary gossip, gleaning London news and producing each day those 'London Letters' professing to come from people with special sources of information. The relationship between the two groups – provincial headquarters and London offices – was friendly; but each felt superior to the other. London considered itself very mighty compared with provincial cities, and the Birmingham group naturally considered itself the master.

The people whom I met in the London office were mainly elderly, for, I was told, the Daily did not like its staff to leave, paid them well and made them comfortable. This and the agreeable 'one of us' welcome I received gave me some confidence. I met an advertisement manager, a business manager, a parliamentary correspondent and the writers of the London Letters. They were fatherly and affable, telling stories of Geo. W. and wishing me joy of Birmingham, laughing a little at the Midlands.

The lady behind the counter came and talked, saying pleasant things about everyone. I was introduced to the two writers of the women's London Letter, each producing three paragraphs in their individual styles a day. I sensed a tension between them. The younger married one was fashionable, attending the Paris shows, fond of dropping French words – *maquillage, bistro* – into her notes, playing the sophisticated woman of the world. The unmarried Miss C. was a historian, fond of describing odd places and people.

She became a friend, and she invited me to lunch and I heard about her struggle to live. She had been one of the pioneering women who had emerged at the beginning of the century. She was Irish and well born and longed to go to a university but never had a chance. In

1910 she had escaped from Ireland and her family and taken a room in London to make a living by her writing. She had nearly starved but gradually had found literary work and now had a good salary from the Daily. She lived with a sister, who wrote historical novels, and they both lavished most of their affection on their cat. She told me that she had never had a love affair and did not think much of men.

Some years later she suddenly resigned from the London Letter. It was partly because of the tension with her companion, but mostly because of the superficiality of journalism. She said she had counted up all the paragraphs she had written in ten years, and there had been hundreds. They had all been pretending that all was for the best in the best of possible worlds, when really the world was full of cruelty and misery.

She went to live with her sister and cat in a cottage in Oxfordshire, and made some small living by book reviewing. She half regretted the move later because she was now poor again. The world would never be very kind to Miss C. She was a feminist before women's equality became part of our national scene.

One thing I noticed about the London staff and later the staff in Birmingham – they were genuine, varied; they did not have to put up a façade as the magazine staff had done. It was almost like being with family friends.

Arrival

I left Euston for Birmingham on an early February afternoon. I called it 'the north' then. I had never been further north than Cambridge, and I was ignorant of Midland geography in a way inconceivable today. Cars and television have at least given later generations an idea of the regions.

The trains of the 1930s were quite speedy, doing the journey in two hours. The afternoon, in an England still pouring out smoke, was dim. The London suburbs, drab but much less spread out than they are today, melted away, and green fields striped with water rolled by. The country was flat, but I noticed fine oaks standing solitary in the fields. Thank God, I thought, trying to find some support in the beauties of nature. They do not desert you. But they did in Birmingham.

We stopped at Rugby and then at Coventry. I noticed red buildings and high chimneys, but twilight had fallen by the time we reached Birmingham. There seemed miles of dirty red brick, slate roofs, dim lights sliding by below us, and then we ran through a black tunnel and stopped. Here was the old New Street Station with its high wooden walkway lined with tin advertisements.

I climbed some steps with the rest of the people, turned along the walkway, saw an exit and asked a man the way to the Daily. He answered obligingly, but I did not understand one word that he said. It was that speech of 'the north'. Luckily the man pointed, and there, up a short sloping street, I saw the corner office with two papers' names in golden letters. So I picked up my case and crossed Birmingham's New Street, that main street that looked like a narrow side road, found myself in front of the office, and pushed a heavy door.

For the first time the glow of light and comfortable warmth received me. I was always to associate that office with warmth as one came in from the cold wet Birmingham streets. A mahogany counter – the sort of grand old-fashioned wood that the Daily would have – was before me and behind it two elderly men, not apparently very busy but benevolent. I half expected the whole thing to be a deception, but Geo. W., they said, was in. They spoke to him on the office telephone, and he said he was waiting for me; and one of the men took me up.

Geo. W. had a larger room than one might have expected for such a modest man. The long windows looked over the dim smoky lights of central Birmingham. I advanced over what seemed miles of carpet and noticed that the room seemed empty. There was a low bookcase with many volumes of the Oxford Dictionary and some reference books and not much else. Geo. W. sat at an almost empty desk. I was to learn that he controlled the paper but did not do much writing himself.

The talk that followed seemed chiefly about my welfare. One of the first questions he asked, drawing at that perpetual cigarette in its holder, was whether I should like to be paid weekly or monthly. I prudently said monthly. Then had I enough money with me? He could offer me a loan. But I was all right. I had brought my small savings.

He had booked me a room at the Grand Hotel 'across the churchyard'. He told me, too, that he had heard of a club for professional women where I might like to live. He stressed, with his old-fashioned prudence, that it was very 'respectable'.

He suggested that I should go and see it the next morning, and come into the office in the evening to meet the staff. This conveniently mapped the day out for me so that I should not have much time to be lonely.

'We work in the evening, you know, but I don't expect you'll have to stay much after ten.' This surprised me. I was so new to journalism that I had not realised that day papers were prepared at night.

I was to learn that Geo. W. himself made a point of leaving exactly at 10.10 every evening in his large car. He pottered in and out of the office in the day, but did not overwhelm himself with work. The rest of the staff, editorial and printing, stayed till 12.55 or later. Then two coaches were waiting, provided by the proprietor, Sir Charles, to do the rounds of Birmingham in different directions and drop people off, one by one. I was soon falling in with this pattern, arriving at 6.30, apart from the odd reporting jobs that I did in the day, and basking in that warm welcoming office for six hours.

Geo. W., after our conversation, took me down some steps and across a wide landing with a settee and a huge oil painting of a tossing sea. I never learned why the painting was there or who was the artist, but the previous owner of the paper, uncle of our Sir Charles, Somebody Feeney, had been a benefactor to the Birmingham Art Gallery and presumably was interested in art.

Across the landing was a room with a desk as littered at Geo. W.'s was empty. Behind it was a man who looked like a diplomat, with a thin handsome face, greying hair and a stoop. This turned out to be Ned, the chief reporter, who worked in the day – a man much loved for his humour. He was said, like so many people in that male office, to be shy of women and he gave me a quizzical glance as we shook hands.

The next-door room was in darkness, but there was a large hairy mat outside the door. Geo. W. switched on the light. 'This is to be yours.' It was a lofty room with a large desk, a swivel chair but as yet no carpet. It looked magnificent to me, but Geo. W. apologised, saying that it was dark but he hoped I should not mind as I should be working in the evening. I was to find that this was a most peculiar honeycomb of a building, added to and changed, and this room had only a swing window up by the ceiling controlled by a long wooden pole with a brass hook. Geo. W. said that he was getting me a carpet, and I was to choose the rest of the furniture myself.

We moved up and down, through winding ways. I was told that

this strange building had had other occupants until recently, but now all of it had been taken over by the three papers of the group – daily, evening and weekly. There were many corners and steps, and the sub-editors' room had no external windows. Presently, after a pilgrimage that bewildered me, we descended to a small back office with another counter – used at night, I was to learn, when the front office was shut – and a door on to a side street. A watchman's box was beside it, and another passage led to unknown depths.

Now I was dismissed for the evening. Geo. W. was very anxious to send a boy to carry my bag and show me the hotel, but I was stupidly shy and said I could find my way perfectly well. He let me have my way, but pointed out the direction, and then I was outside in the cold wet night. Birmingham always does seem bleak after London.

I trailed up a narrow street, discovered an opening in railings, found myself in a central grassy space with tombstones, and saw in front of me across a street the lights of the Grand Hotel. I went in and was conducted to a narrow room, and suddenly all was quiet about me.

Feeling as if I had just finished an examination, I wrote a postcard to my family.

Evening Exploration

I had a solitary meal at the hotel, and then there was the evening before me.

I knew absolutely nothing about the shape and lay-out of Birmingham, and only later was to learn that it was composed of a series of linked villages. Any sensible person would have bought a plan or map, but many people were largely oblivious of the plans of places in those pre-television days. I came, in any case, from an unobservant family with a poor sense of direction.

I decided to go out and discover the city. It was dark and seemed dimly lit, but in those days we had no fear of street attacks. Britain was said to be the only country where girls could walk alone safely at night. I had no idea if the hotel was in the centre of the town. It seemed not with those railings and that grassy space with its tombstones. I had been brought up near the Thames and one thing I could not imagine was a large city without a river. But at least, I thought, there would be a main street.

I must have wandered some miles on that first evening, round and round. A sharp mist was now over the soaking streets. I went up and down looking for that central thoroughfare, but everywhere there seemed to be only a narrow maze. There were no lighted frontages of any importance, but the place seemed hilly, with the dark grassy churchyard at the top.

I found a tall château-like building, very Victorian, which seemed to be a Post Office. I plunged down a steep hill beside it, thinking that Birmingham's centre might be down there. But the street seemed only to lead to shabby little shops; so I came up again to the hill and tried the opposite direction. I found another large railway station and another street leading down by a line of black arches. Steamy poor little shop windows had notes about dishes called 'faggot and peas', of which I had never heard. I came to a wide right turning with tall looming chimneys and a cobbled wet waste, and still the hunched dirty brick buildings spread away on every side. Later I was to tramp Summer Lane weekly as I went down to collect pennies for the Birmingham Settlement; but now it looked like a black slum.

So I went up again and with a sense of relief found the churchyard and door of the hotel with its padded warmth. I had nobody to talk to; so I went early to bed.

Mayfield

The streets were still wet the next morning, but there was a glint of sun, and from the hotel window I watched a crowd of people who seemed rather shabby passing up and down the street. Behind them was the modest eighteenth-century shape of the church which, I was to find, was called 'the cathedral', and black bare trees.

Geo. W. had said that the women's club was expecting me and I was to catch a Number 4 cream bus to reach it. I emerged with the feeling of detachment such as one has on holiday.

The cream bus passed a pillared building which I was to know later as the Town Hall, designed by Joseph Hansom, inventor of the 'patent safety cab'. As the bus turned right I saw a peculiar pale dome which, I was to learn, was Birmingham's useless and odd war memorial. Birmingham was certainly not a 'city of the arts' in those days.

On the bus went, past low shops, generally built on to the frontages of older houses, and finally came to a junction of many roads with a Victorian clock and a long triangle of grass which made a small public garden. Then we suddenly entered a different world – a world that my mother was later to compare with Bournemouth – with large trees arching their branches over the road and large red brick houses standing back behind drives and gardens. We were in Edgbaston, home of the well-to-do successful manufacturers, many of them Quakers.

'Mayfield', the women's club, was one of the large houses, but it seemed to have passed its best days. It stood behind old trees with a semi-circle of moss-grown drive. Its wide doorstep was greened with lichen, and its paint was peeling. There was dim stained glass in its door.

A bright small woman, looking like an elf with an Eton crop, opened the door. She was expecting me, she said in her chirpy voice, and she smiled merrily. Luckily she had one room free.

The big shabby house was quiet at the moment as most of the residents were professional women and were out working. The elf took me up some stairs with a worn carpet and into a narrow room which had obviously been cut from a larger bedroom. 'Yours,' she said, and that was comforting. Out of the window I could see a huge garden with a spread of lawn and a magnificent beech.

'You will be quite the baby,' the elf said, and she took me downstairs and showed me a vast room also looking out on to the garden. 'We have coffee in here. Some of my children – I call them my children – have gardens of their own. You may have one too if you like.'

It was all settled in a moment. The terms were quite stiff for those days, but I could easily manage them out of my eight pounds a week. The elf did not mind my odd working hours. 'Some of us are in for lunch, and you can join us, and I can leave you an egg for your supper when you come in late. I'll give you a key.'

It all seemed very easy. I returned to the hotel, which had been a refuge but was now of no particular interest, paid my bill and picked up my bag. Already I seemed to have been in Birmingham for days.

Meeting Staff

I had been bidden to call in at the Daily office at six. I found the back office in its side street, felt the warmth and brightness, saw a grinning young man behind the counter and was directed up the stairs to my room with its hairy doormat.

I switched on the light and saw that the room now had a thick grey-blue carpet with a small pink flower pattern – certainly an expensive covering. But it was an odd room with a massive hat and umbrella stand in a corner and the long pole with the brass hook leaning against the wall. A large electric fire stood in the hearth where there had once been a coal fire, and a large metal waste-paper bin stood by the large desk with its swivel chair.

I found Geo. W. in his room and showed him my poor harvest of articles. He was as usual agreeable. A few he gently rejected. 'No-o-o hardly. Not the right sort of subject.' But most could go 'upstairs'. Would I get them ready for the printers? The head printer would talk to me about headings and types.

But most of that evening was given to a long tour of the maze of rooms and many introductions to smirking men, who were embarrassed to have Geo. W. seek them out and to have to greet this invading woman. One of the few absentees was Sir Charles, owner of the paper. 'Charlie', a melancholy but generous bachelor, reputed to be a millionaire, was always on the Riviera at this time of year.

I was to hear more of 'Charlie' from the printers. His uncle, from whom he had inherited the papers, had been a hard businessman, but Charlie had not had to struggle and he showed great paternal generosity to his work force. He paid more than the trade-union wage. In the summer he arranged a garden party on his country estate and in the winter a dinner and dance at the Grand Hotel. He had provided a canteen for the staff at the top of the building so that the printers could have a hot supper. 'Charlie – he's a gentleman,' they would say.

A few years before, however, there had been a dilemma. In 1926 had occurred the General Strike, when trade-union leaders had ordered their followers to support the miners and refuse to work. 'We didn't want to strike – not against Charlie,' the men said. But they had to follow trade-union policy, and they struck, and editors, sub-editors, and reporters worked the machines and brought out a single sheet of news each morning. Charlie had felt bitter afterwards and had withdrawn some of his benefits, such as the generous pensions scheme. But now four years had passed, and peace reigned, and he was bringing back his philanthropic arrangements. However, memories of the strike lingered. I heard of it from both editorial staff and printers.

Good temper now reigned in the building, though not all the 'nobs' were liked. The papers' financial manager inspired fear – a hard red-faced white-haired man much given to speaking on charitable platforms but also to squeezing the waists of any girls in the office. This, however, was regular behaviour from elderly bosses at the time, and the girls suffered it because they were afraid of the colonel (although he was only a colonel in the Boys' Brigade). Anyhow he worked in the day, and the night staff did not see much of him.

From the first the office seemed a haven of comfort. Perhaps it was too comfortable, for the staff stayed on and grew elderly. The Daily's circulation was never very high, and it was paid for by the sister evening paper, which was more popular in tone and made more of sport. The Daily's static circulation was one of the reasons for the 'Women's Interests' page and of my appearance. I was told the story later by the head printer.

Round the Office

Geo. W. took me up some stairs and opened a door. The room was thick with cigarette smoke, and one of two men were standing before sloping desks. They jumped to attention and shook hands in an embarrassed way. Geo. W. explained that they were reporters and might sometimes supply material for my page.

At the top of the stairs in a room with high bookcases of new shiny books was old Joe, the literary editor. His name was not Joe, but his surname was Gorman, and there had been an entertainer Joe Gorman and so the office had nicknamed him. He was not like an entertainer or indeed like a literary editor – a white-haired erect man with a heavy moustache, a high old-fashioned collar and a gold-rimmed monocle. His manner was elaborately courteous.

He had become book editor in a roundabout way, which also showed that literature did not rank high with the Daily. He had been born in India and worked for an Indian paper, and later when he came to England had been taken on by the Daily to write an occasional leader on India. To fill up the gaps between the leaders he had been given charge of the books and the review page once a week.

I do not think old Joe was a great student of books, but for that reason he may have been a good literary editor. He belonged to no faction. He had no axe to grind. He was extremely polite and benevolent to the outside reviewers, mainly the academics of Birmingham itself, who in the evening tramped up the stairs to get books from him.

Geo. W. suggested that from time to time there might be a book that I could deal with in 'Women's Interests'. 'Certainly,' old Joe said. He was as good as his word, bringing down cookery books, biographies of famous women and, before Christmas, armfuls of girls' stories for the special book supplement.

At the end of the evening I had the vaguest idea of the office staff, but they soon became distinct figures. There were three leader writers, with rooms opening on to the landing with the huge sea picture. Two were Oxford men, but the deputy editor was non-Oxford – Mr L.P.H., a solid literary figure who had been with the paper for many years and had a tall benevolent wife concerned with Birmingham charities. L.P.H. was much respected, but he might have done better if he had not been so comfortable and had moved on. But here, I was to discover later, was a problem of provincial cities. They had not enough journalistic openings to allow many people to occupy the top places, and people who had roots in the city and children at school there, and so did not want to move, were stuck in one job. In the 'thirties there were not all those extra jobs in local television and local radio.

Each leader writer of the Daily had his speciality. L.P.H. dealt with British news. Another man did foreign news, and the third did odd subjects and humour. The third looked after the 'obits', biographies of well-known people kept ready for their deaths. 'Obits' had to be constantly revised and added to. The leader writers also reviewed books, going up to old Joe's room and, without much reference to him, taking what they wanted. Like Geo. W. they wrote their pieces in longhand. Another of their jobs was to read proofs.

There were rivalries between them, but on that first night they were very agreeable, and I looked on them with awe. As a woman I could never reach their heights.

Then we moved on to the sub-editors' department, cut from an inner corner of that rambling building and like a schoolroom. In the teacher's big desk facing the others was the chief sub-editor, Mr T. He was a little like a younger Churchill but had a glass eye after being wounded in the Great War and, like most of them, a heart of gold. In lines facing him were his men. Mr T. received the news material that came in to the paper, read it, threw away much and handed out the rest to his henchmen who put in punctuation and headings. From the sub-editors the news went up to the printers.

The sub-editors were a mixed group with varied personalities, for under beneficent rule individualities can flourish. George, the second-in-command, with bright brown eyes and early white hair, was merry and able to turn his hand to anything, as he had been in the Navy. In and out fussed old Jack, the handyman, generally followed by a pimply youth. Jack brought the news bags up from the station, did odd jobs, and spent much time swearing and in an artificial fury. He had a drooping moustache and was about five feet tall. A serious young man, pillar of the local chapel, was the sports editor.

Our last visit of the evening was to the composing room. I was not to prepare my first page till the Sunday night, but Geo. W. thought I should look at the printers, as they would make up the women's page. We climbed to the composing room and reading room up a steep metal staircase which reminded me of a ship's stairs. At the top on the left were swing doors, and we pushed through to meet a blaze of light. Small men with white aprons scurried about with long trays of type or silvery blocks of advertisements on their shoulders. Others stood at racks picking out letters with tweezers and making lines of type. Others bent over long silvery tables with heavy metal frames to make up pages.

An open staircase at the back led up again to the processing rooms for photographs, always, I was to think, with the smell of my old school laboratory. But I did not go up there on that first formal evening. To one side were two monster presses with the name of a Berne firm. They provided flat page proofs before the heavy oblong of type was turned into a semi-circular metal block to go into the rotary machines for printing. Near by was the head printer's 'box' – a small wooden chamber up steps. Here he hung his coat, kept papers, ate his supper and supervised the work when he was not striding about.

The head printer was known at Wag, as his name was W. A. Griffith.

He met us with smiles and a little polite voice much milder than his tones when he bawled at the printers in hectic moments. A tall man, very different from most of the printers who were small, he was in early middle age, with a black moustache and an air of competence. He was very gracious that night, promising help in his small polite voice. I did not understand all he said for, though he claimed to be descended from Welsh kings, he had a strong Black Country accent, and he could not sound his Rs. He was to puzzle me later by saying that I had 'furr urr' and to offer me 'purrs' from his garden.

For years I was to work with Wag, and found him generally very efficient and kindly. But he was not popular with the men; he shouted at them too much. And in a crisis he tended to be treacherous, pushing the blame on to someone else. Yet we all relied on him.

There was much to see in the composing room, and, early in the evening before the rush of getting pages out, Wag would sometimes take visitors round, being very gracious. The room had a long narrow space, at the bottom of which were the linotype machines, operated by men sitting and touching keys lightly to turn molten metal into lines of print. It was always warm down there, and they were among the star turns of the room, explaining the machines' intricacies – which visitors did not understand – and finally asking for names. Then they would gently touch their keys and bring out a hot silvery line of letters which spelt out the name, but backward of course, so that it could be dabbed on to an ink pad and make a right-way impression. One by one the visitors received their names in metal and these were souvenirs of the composing-room tour.

But that first evening I was only vaguely aware of all the activities – the men smiling and saying good evening, the racks of galleys and the silvery surfaces. There seemed a vast amount of bustle, and soon I was to learn the importance of time in running a daily paper.

After tripping through the departments, looking through post and having a visit from Wag to show me how to prepare articles for Sunday night, I was dismissed at about ten and told to return on Sunday for the first issue of 'Women's Interests'. A heading for the page had been designed by Wag.

Furniture Interlude

'If you call on Mr Robinson,' Geo. W. had said to me, 'he will see about the furniture for your room.'

I had thought that my lofty apartment was already furnished, but I was afraid to ask questions. On the Saturday morning I went down to the office to find Mr Robinson, known as 'Piggy'. He was a roly-poly old man with white hair, and the nickname distinguished him from another Robinson in the firm. Piggy Robinson was in charge of the office furnishing.

He came out at once and escorted me along New Street to a furniture shop which my family would have considered over-expensive. All the time he was apologising for giving me trouble. 'We put the ordinary things in your room, but the editor thought you would like some extras. A young lady must have a mirror of course.'

I was astonished. Why were they being so nice? Was there some catch? But it seemed there was not. Gradually, as time went on, I was to take the kindness of the office for granted and to assert that 'everyone is good at heart'. Some of the benevolence was no doubt due to my youth and sex, but it also was part of the office itself – then but not later. Later I was to revise my glib confidence in the goodness of human nature.

I chose as plain a mirror as I could, though Piggy would have paid for a decorated frame. 'You ask now for what you want,' he said. 'They may not be so willing to spend money on you later.'

He led me to the chair department. 'A young lady needs an armchair.' This seemed more waste of money, and I said that my swivelling desk chair was enough. But Piggy insisted. 'The editor said we were to make you comfortable.'

So I selected an expensive and soft chair with wide arms. 'And now what about the covering?' Piggy insisted. 'You'll want your own covering.'

I had never heard of such extravagance. The chair had some inconspicuous floral covering that was quite acceptable. But Piggy beckoned the salesman and asked for a book of materials, and, still with a feeling that I might be dreaming, I chose a velvety blue-grey material. 'Get it done as quickly as possible for the young lady,' Piggy ordered. I noted that the shop treated him with deference. I suppose the Daily ran up large bills there.

The armchair, beautifully covered, arrived in a few days and occupied a corner by the hearth in my room. I used to throw papers on to it when I had a full desk. The only time I sat in it was on dark November Saturday afternoons when I came into the deserted office to work on the piles of girls' stories that I had to review for the Christmas book pages.

'Now a safe,' Piggy announced.

'A *safe?*'

'Young ladies have valuables, don't they? You'll want a safe place for locking things up.'

'I shan't have any valuables at the office,' I protested, but it was no good. He just said, 'You have a safe while you can,' and asked to see specimens. He bought me a large green metal safe with a mighty key. It went into my cupboard, and I forgot it.

I enjoyed a double honour that morning – the shop so deferential to Piggy and Piggy so generous to me. I felt like a princess, but was still not quite sure if my royalty would last.

Looking for the Country

I made a fool of myself at Mayfield, the women's hostel, on the Sunday. I was to go into the Daily office at six, but had the morning and afternoon free and knew nobody to talk to. So I thought at 10.30 that I would go out to the country. Lunch was at one. I should have plenty of time.

In those days before television and the increased importance of the provinces, people from the south of England tended to think that everything outside London was 'country'. We knew that there were large towns but thought of them as only small patches in the billowing fields.

Mayfield was not far from Five Ways with its clock and triangle of grass, and I knew that the roads there led into town. So I went the opposite way, westward, along quiet curving thoroughfares with tree branches spreading over high fences. It seemed that at any moment I might come to fields.

I did come to some botanical gardens which seemed to have wide spaces. Perhaps this was the beginning of the country. It was a raw

February morning, chilly and grey among the houses, but over fields, I thought, there might be a touch of spring.

I must have walked for two hours at least. The big houses with their trees and drives were succeeded by small red brick properties, but I probably walked in circles anyhow. Then I turned into a side street and saw at the end – a tram.

In those days trams ran along most of the main roads out of the centre of Birmingham. To me they were a symbol of town life. They meant that the fields for which I was looking were illusions. I followed the side street to the long main road, and then had to ask the way back to Mayfield, catch a tram and then walk. It was 1.30 when I arrived back, half an hour late for lunch. When I explained that I had been looking for fields the ladies, who were having coffee in the large room, laughed.

There seemed about a dozen of them, all rather old. I had already seen some of them. Through the following weeks I got to know them better, but always with the feeling that I was out of it. The oldest was a large deaf white-haired lady who, I was told, had been governess to the children of a bishop of Birmingham. She was now retired; was one of the earliest residents of Mayfield and had special terms. What she did with her time I did not know. Most of the others were professional women out during the day – teachers, social workers, medical staff. The humorist of the company, described as a 'scream', was a fat merry woman who ran an employment agency and was also the star of an amateur theatrical group. Her jokes at meal times made the other ladies roar with laughter – all except the deaf ex-governess and myself who did not understand the local references. The youngest resident until I arrived was a fair pale woman aged twenty-eight who did some teaching and belonged to the strong Quaker community in Birmingham. The others spoke of her with pity. She had been ill and had had, it was said, some unfortunate love affair. But she was not in very much.

Since I was at work in the evening I had only one meal, lunch, with the company. I found these meals rather an ordeal as I was shy and a stranger to Birmingham. I was known as 'little Miss Freeman'.

I do not think there are many clubs like Mayfield today. The women would either be married or in flats. Mayfield meant a certain separation from the world, though you could have friends in and book rooms for entertaining. The elf who ran the place called the residents her 'children', which implied a freedom from all domestic responsibility. As spring came I was to find the mornings, with no domestic jobs, rather empty.

That all was not well with the house itself I was to find on my first late return from work. The elf had said she would put an egg and bread and butter ready for my supper, and I was to go to the kitchen to get the tray.

When I came in after midnight the house was in darkness and silence except for faint snores coming from one of the bedrooms. I crept in, cautiously switched on the hall light, and stole down the stairs to the basement kitchen.

Mayfield, a Victorian building, had a series of large rooms down there, with brick floors and a musty smell. When I switched on the light I found the place alive with black beetles (cockroaches), millions, it seemed, swarming over floors and tables. When the light went on they disappeared in a second, but of course they would come back when I retreated. Luckily the tray was covered.

I had never seen such a host of beetles before. For a moment I felt sick. But there was nothing I could do; so I took my tray and turned the light off and left them to reassemble. I suppose the elf knew about them, but, as was to appear later, the house needed endless repairs and she had not the money to pay for them. I was too shy to complain of the cockroaches, and presently I became almost used to them. After all it was not their fault, I thought, that they had been born.

Night Work

Evening workers for the Daily went in by the entry up a narrow side street since the front office was closed. That first evening, coming in from the chill and dimness, I was aware of warmth and gold light. Behind the counter of the back office was a grinning young man whom I was to know as Bert, who gave the impression that he would do anything for anybody. He was an ally of old Jack, the small swearing man-of-all-work. Sometimes Bert and Jack would visit my room together and Bert would show Jack off, accusing him of great wealth, and Jack would ball his fists and pretend to be furious.

Soon I learnt the winding way to my room with its large hairy doormat. The evening with its varied jobs – one of the advantages of managing something on one's own – soon fell into a pattern. There were always contributions in long envelopes sent for 'Women's Interests' in the shiny wooden tray, solid like the rest of the furnishings. On top of my typewriter, new and supplied by the office, were six long sheets with lines of purple capital letters – the Women's London Letter. At first they arrived as tapes stuck to paper, supplied by our cubbyhole of a wireroom, still communicating with London by Morse code; but by an improvement afterwards the letter was printed directly on to paper. I had to prepare the sheets for the printers, reading for sense and marking in the punctuation and capital letters.

It was not as easy as it appeared. Odd mistakes came through, sixes and nines turned upside-down, figures reversed as in 1518 for Waterloo. The United States generally arrived as 'Untied States', and letters got transposed, as once when I dealt with a note on Japanese screens. These were said to be sold in Paris and I marked the capital P and thought no more of it. But the next day there came a complaint from London that the screens should have been sold in *pairs*.

Sometimes the ladies themselves made mistakes. I remember one complaining that nobody could spell 'Wedgewood'. I began to hurry to the long line of Encyclopaedia Britannicas in the next-door room of Ned, the chief reporter, to check facts. There is always a little tension between the writer and the sub-editor who deals with the material, and now and then there would be mild complaints from London. On the other hand I did occasionally get thanks when I spotted some mistake.

I had to work quickly as the London Letter had to be printed before the pressure of news-printing began. A messenger would come and carry the sheets away. Then I had to think of pictures, which varied according to the number of advertisements on the page. I went in to Ned's room, and he would be sitting with a pile of photographs in front of him – those taken by our own photographers and those that had come by train from London. When Ned grew used to me we would get a good deal of amusement from the photographs. He would hand me silently the print of a fat lady with her skirt blowing up or of a member of the Royal Family with a crooked scowl. Once he handed me the picture of a dark elegant lady on a golf course. The caption said it was Mrs Simpson.

'Mrs Simpson?' I said, puzzled.

'The lady,' Ned said. He was always sparing with words.

I had to choose possible pictures for 'Women's Interests'. But what exactly were women's interests? Events concerning women, of course, as long as they were not too important. And I was allowed 'pretty pictures' as we called them – the first lambs, the first snowdrops in the woods, a child smelling tulips in a park. If there was nothing suitable among the day's gleanings I would fall back on fashion photographs sent by a London agency. My trouble with these was that they were often long and narrow so that one had to find a very brief heading. A man 'up the road', as we called our rival group of papers, told me that when he dealt with pictures of fashions, of which he knew nothing, he always headed them 'Smart and Neat'.

Soon after I arrived in the evening Wag would appear with a neatly ruled slip of paper showing me the arrangement of my page for the night. He would go afterwards to Geo. W. with a small folded dummy of the whole paper. My make-up plans would depend on the advertisements, in blocks at the sides. Indeed the whole paper was governed by them, and was small on Monday, a poor day, and specially small in the 'silly season' of July and August, but large, running to twenty pages, on Saturdays, the best day for advertisements.

'You won't 'ave much room tonight,' Wag would say with a grin when advertisements were large. For the paper's revenues depended not on admiring readers but on commercial patronage. But on those prosperous days I would be disappointed, as there would be less space for my material.

I would go with a choice of five or six photographs to Geo. W. after he had seen Wag. I always had a feeling of unease on these visits, for if the editor was one of the shy ones so was I. 'No-o, I hardly think . . .' he would say. 'Well, try these two.' His judgement was always measured. He had been a journalist for too long to have any strong feelings except his dislike of London. And he always professed profound ignorance concerning 'the ladies' though he had had two wives.

I would take the chosen photographs back to my room to cut and mark reductions. Then I would write the captions. Being young and highbrow I tried to offer an occasional poetic heading, such as Keats's 'Green-robed senators of mighty woods' for a forest scene. I also tried to write informative captions. Once when, short of pictures, we used a photograph of the preparation of snuff as a quaint survival, I looked the subject up and explained that 'snuff is a form of tobacco'. The enigmatic Mr L.P.H., the deputy editor, who wrote in a crabbed hand and always used green ink, would come into my room when I was absent and leave sarcastic notes on my desk. After I had informed the public of obvious facts about snuff I found the cut out picture on my desk and the additional note in green ink, 'and tobacco is an Indian weed.' Neither of us alluded to these sarcasms.

Actually I found to my surprise that many of the older printers and other took snuff, which could be bought at a small shop up our side street. It was a substitute for cigarettes, for the printers were not allowed to smoke in the composing room because of fire danger. Old Jack, of the drooping moustache and the tempers, used to carry a snuff-box round with him and stand in front of my desk to sniff up the brown powder with an air of intense enjoyment. He was always begging me to try some, and once I did, and tears rushed to my eyes and I choked. Then he doubled up in merriment.

But that was later when we all knew each other well.

Evening Hours

The leader writers arrived at seven. The three of them assembled with Geo. W. in his room, and his door was shut and a hush fell on the landing. They were discussing what subjects were to be taken for leaders, and it all seemed secret and important, and I, of course, as a woman was excluded. After about ten minutes the door would open and steps would sound on the landing. There would be a word or two, and then the writers would go to their rooms and silence descended again as they wrote their pieces.

But they did not all write every night, and sometimes they would come into my room for a brief conversation. That early evening was a time for visitors – reviewers coming in to tramp up the stairs to old Joe's room for books, reporters dropping in to my room with pieces they thought might do for 'Women's Interests' – rather embarrassing this sometimes if the pieces were not very good – outside contributors coming in to discuss articles. But long visits were not encouraged as the production of the paper depended on speed.

Sometimes Florrie came down to see me from the height of the picture processing rooms. She was very pleasant, and we felt a bond of womanhood among all those men. But at first, not knowing her name, I called her 'the nigger lady' in the blithe way of pre-immigration days. I was rebuked by the printers who told me her name and were friends with her. Her father had been black while her mother was a pale white-haired Birmingham woman. In the 'thirties Florrie with her dark skin was a target for rudeness. She once told a printer that she had suffered so much that she could suffer no more.

She had a brother who, as might be expected, was more easily received than she. He worked for a local firm and was married. Florrie herself was a good charitable typical unmarried woman, doing various voluntary jobs such as the collection for National Savings. But her job in the office was unusual, and I never heard how she had got it. Working with a brush and brown watercolour she was a toucher-up of photographs before they were printed. She would strengthen a line or block in a pale background to make objects stand out. Press photographs were not as expert at today's – and of course uncoloured – and they often needed improvement. Florrie's results often looked crude, but she did generally clarify the image. She worked for both morning and evening papers and would stay in the evening for the Daily's batch and then go home.

At 7.30 I had a regular visit from a canteen lady with a tray. The printers went to the canteen, which was up another steep flight of stairs, at 7.45; so the ladies looked after me before they were too busy. When one first came down to ask what I would like for my supper I had no idea what to say, but they pressed me to have something and in the end suggested bread and butter and a cake. In fact they brought, with perfect regularity through the years, two slices of new white bread with very yellow butter, two garish cakes – 'We put aside the best for you' – and a glass of cold milk. (The milk later, in the war, was to cause me acute indigestion.) I had no idea whether I was supposed to pay for this bounty, but thought it better to offer. They said that they didn't know what to charge; but would sixpence a night be all right? I suppose I should have offered more, but I didn't know the ways of the office. It remained sixpence a night until I left.

The three canteen ladies were great favourites with the men – comely women, dispensers of meals and in themselves good-looking and kind. Two were sisters – another Florrie and Lucy – Junoesque women with large bosoms. 'Our Florrie's a good armful,' the printers would say. Florrie and Lucy had grown-up children about whom they used to talk. The third canteen lady was unmarried, smaller and darker but also amiable. It was a long journey through the office to reach me each night, and they came back for the tray later. But by this time I was growing so used to being treated kindly that I probably did not thank them enough.

Also during the evening a reader might come down with a query. Though in the composing room I was allowed to break trade-union rules, which absolutely excluded women from the printing trade, and I occasionally looked in the racks for galleys of news I wanted, the readers' room was completely barred to me. It was high up, near the composing room, and guarded by a white-haired courteous and adamant chief reader. If I wanted to discuss anything he would come out, bar the door and send the man I wanted out to me. Through the doorway I would have only a brief impression of men with green eye-shades working in pairs under bright lights, one whisperingly reading from a proof and the other marking in corrections.

So the readers often came down to me. They were our good angels. Each of the editorial staff was given a dictionary and a style book, but we all had our aberrations. The readers, unfailingly polite, found the mistakes that slipped through, and were especially good on dates. One would come down humbly and ask if Edward VII were not dead by 1910, and they were nearly always right.

They failed in two ways. In those insular days they could not manage foreign languages, which often appeared because I had travel articles; and they left foreign words to me. They also could not understand that we sometimes had intentional mistakes. I might put in a quotation from a charwoman's letter, 'I cant com no moare,' and the reader would correct it. I would mark it back again to bad spelling. Then a humble man would come down and ask if the quotation was not faulty. I would explain that it was meant to be so, but like as not another reader would get hold of the proof and correct it again.

Sometimes I myself became a joke. Wag explained to me the type the paper used – small and insignificant in those days. 'Egyptian' was the type for headings of short pieces. I did not hear properly and sent up pieces with the heading marked 'Gyp'. My copy was passed round and the men went red in the face with laughter.

But I was not the only one. One leader writer, who was considered 'superior' and not much liked, had an aberration one evening and in his academic writing crossed out 'sandwich' on a proof and wrote in 'samwich'. This too was passed round with laughter and put up on the printers' notice-board.

In between the visits I would get on with the regular tasks. Articles printed the night before had to be marked up for payment. We generously paid half-a-crown an inch, excluding headings, and I was allowed to spend up to eight pounds a night. Only once Geo. W. asked me if I were not being a little extravagant, but I showed him that I had never gone over the mark. I was too timid for that. The sum owing and the name of the contributor went into a large ruled ledger, and once a month a tall polite spectacled young man came in the day and carried the ledger away and made out cheques. This simple system, depending on a minimum of red tape, pleased our contributors who remarked on the Daily's promptness.

There were contributions to be read and kept or sent back. Sometimes parcels had to be done up. At first I did my own, but then old Jack would appear, take a glance, swear, stamp out and return with brown paper and string to re-do my loose effort. He was the most perfect parcel-maker I have ever met, and in the end I left all packets to him.

Messengers from the composing room would come down with long trails of proofs, one column wide. I would have one proof and the readers another, and I would keep the corrected versions in a drawer to be used for the page. Each evening I had to plan a page, taking care that the articles were not too much alike. Geo. W. allowed me to have initials underneath; nothing more personal.

At 8.45, when the men were back from the canteen, I took my bundle of proofs and went up to the composing room. For an hour or so I worked with a printer at the long silvery metal slab, still called a 'stone'. The heavy oblong metal chase (frame) would be there, the column rules in place, with block advertisements at the sides or with the places where they were to go marked. Pictures would seldom be ready, but their spaces would be marked. The evening's London Letter, now in type, would be brought up. Then I had to fill in the spaces with articles.

I worked at the opposite side of the stone to the printer. I soon learnt to read the backward metal type, printed in lines, and the tricks of making things fit. If one had to cut, it should be at the end of the paragraph to avoid the necessity of much re-setting. Bits of lines could be nipped off with pincers. If the piece was a little too short it could be 'bumped out' with more space in the heading and thin copper slips between the lines.

Recipes, which secretly I detested, were useful for filling in small spaces. But we generally had to find small pieces of news too. These had to be of a special kind. No murder or crime was possible of course. 'Midland Wills' were favoured because they had a touch of eternity about them, and other things that were slightly non-newsy might do. Charities and good deeds were welcome, especially if they involved women.

The page had to be finished and 'away' by ten so that it did not hinder the news-setting. The chase was screwed up and two proofs were taken on the flat presses near by. The readers had one proof and I had one which I took down to the editor, who would be about to depart. It was like going through an examination each night, and I always felt tremulous, though he generally made no comment. Then I myself looked through the page, and always found something I should like to alter. But generally I restrained myself as time was short.

The flat spread of print and pictures finally went away to be turned into a curved block of metal to go on the big rotary machines in the bowels of the building. It seemed that a great deal of trouble was taken for something as ephemeral as a newspaper page, but there were always people to criticise – perhaps more so because the Daily was a local paper. 'As I was reading the paper for mistakes . . .' one man wrote. He complained that the women's page had talked of a twenty-first birthday, when really everyone has only one day of birth. 'You had better make it "anniversary of a birthday" in future,' Geo. W. said wearily.

End of the Evening

In the hours leading to midnight, time flies. I soon found that I was not ready to go at ten o'clock as Geo. W. had expected. There were too many jobs, and I wrote articles myself because I liked writing and wanted to keep costs down. Birmingham buses stopped at something after eleven, and so I waited for the office coaches that lined up in the side street at about 12.30.

Geo. W. did not interfere at all. I think now he must have been remarkably easy-going with a girl employee in her early twenties. One of the pleasures of the office was that you had so little supervision.

At about ten the leader writers finished their pieces, and two of them went out to a local pub for a drink. Geo. W.'s room was dark except for lamplight from the street, and most of the reporters would have gone except for one on late duty who rang round to hospitals and police stations at midnight to find if anything unusual had happened. While upstairs in the composing room the pace increased to get the first edition out by something after midnight, we would relax on our landing, the leader writers doing odd jobs and reading the daily London papers that came to them. Sometimes, if I had no jobs, I would borrow the papers to see what was happening in the far-off metropolis. Not that we cared for London!

Important news sometimes was due at awkward times. Just after I had arrived the office was agog because the Duchess of York, having had a girl, Elizabeth, was in her second labour, unaware probably that she was keeping newspapers hanging on for the announcement of the birth. Would it be a boy? It was not.

Later Hitler's speeches, at which we held our breaths, arrived inconveniently late. On the other hand a death – which I remember because of the mysterious remarks outside my door – was reported in mid-evening. I heard one of the leader writers saying, 'Don't tell Miss Freeman,' and I wondered what on earth had happened. It was the death of D. H. Lawrence, accepted by Cambridge as a genius and therefore one of my enthusiasms. I must have made myself a bore by talking about him.

Midnight would come. My room would be comfortable and warm. Upstairs the fever would have cooled a little as the first edition of the paper had gone down to the machines. It should be ready by about 12.30 and would be rushed across country in a van to a station to meet a particular stopping London train. Most of the printers would go home in the two coaches, but a group would stop to print emergency and late news for the second and third editions. Like other morning papers, the Daily travelled further than its evening sister, and it penetrated nearly as far as Bristol.

We ourselves, the evening over, filed out by the side entrance. As we passed, one of the machine men would hand to each of us the next day's paper. The coaches would be waiting in the narrow street, one to go south and east and the other west and north. We all had our special seats. In my coach two leader writers would sit side by side in front, cut off from the multitude and talking desultorily of mutual acquaintances. I sat behind them with a middle-aged silent printer who, I am sure, was embarrassed by my presence. Behind, the rest of the printers crowded, very cheerful now work was finished. Joking conversation flew to and fro, with football and gardening among the main subjects. The Arsenal and Aston Villa seemed to my ignorant ears to be chiefly bandied about. 'Well, Harry,' somebody would begin, 'who's agoing to win on Saturday?' and there would be great arguments and jokes about the players. Or, to a noted gardener, 'Tommy, how are the onions?' and then there would be assertions that Tommy liked gardening only because it gave him a chance to hunt slugs and 'do the creepy-crawlies in'.

Street lighting cannot have been very good, for there seemed to be black darkness outside the coach windows, with one or two brilliant visions in the lamplight – a branch outlined in snow, a red flowering currant bush which I looked for in one garden every spring. The coach would stop at fixed places, and one printer after another would climb down with loud goodnights. In my later days when I had a flat far up the long Hagley Road I would alight with a tall talkative man who walked a few paces with me making conversation before he turned into a side road. I used to wonder if his strident tones would wake all those sleepers behind curtained windows. When we parted with yet another goodnight I went on a few paces, cautiously let myself in at my own front door, mounted to my flat, turned on the gas fire and spread the paper on the floor to read the news. I made myself a meal after that, and it was generally four o'clock before I got to bed. Most of us found that we needed a cooling-off time before we slept.

To Stratford

'Perhaps you will spend Sunday with us,' Geo. W. said soon after I arrived. He was still trying to make me feel at home.

In my week or two in Birmingham I had learnt something about him. Everybody trusted 'the old man', but he was rather a solitary figure with his beard, spare form and long cigarette-holder. He had begun as a reporter in the Midlands, and stayed there, hating London. He had risen gradually, become editor of the evening paper attached to the Daily and then had been appointed editor of the Daily itself.

I heard stories of his troubles. His diabetic son had been a 'weed' who had died in his late teens. The bossy wife had died too, and now Geo. W. had married her sister, and they lived in leafy Harborne which still kept a little of its country character. Human nature is always surprising, and Geo. W. was interested in two things – motoring and dancing.

He was, I suppose, a man of narrow interests, but he was not closed to new ideas. Wag, the head printer, told me, with a certain self-satisfaction, how my appointment had come about. The Daily's head printer had retired through ill health, and the Daily printers had hoped that one of them would get the job. But Geo. W. had chosen Wag, the head printer 'up the road', with the rival more popular group of papers. Wag was a man of great energy, inclined to be conceited, vulnerable but highly efficient, and he had advised on ways in which the Daily circulation could be stimulated. One of his suggestions was a woman's page. Geo. W. had agreed.

It would be an ordeal, I felt, to have hospitality from the boss, but life was all ordeal in those first days in Birmingham. I arrived for lunch at a warm brick house on a cold February Sunday, and the meal was made easy by a small talkative wife who had come from Wales. She talked constantly of Deganwy, and I disguised the fact that I did not know exactly where the place was. After lunch Geo. W. asked if I would like a 'run' to look at the Midlands.

The 'run' was one of the most illuminating geography lessons that I ever had. We dressed ourselves up, for, though Geo. W. had an expensive car – I was too ignorant of motoring to note the make – it, like all other cars, had no heating. At the back were piles of rugs. I was seated with Mrs Geo. W. in the back seats, and we muffled ourselves up, but even then we soon grew stiff.

'What about Stratford?' said Geo. W.

I was astonished. Stratford-on-Avon? Shakespeare's Stratford? I had not had the slightest idea that it was near Birmingham; but then I had never much thought where it was anyhow. Now I was to learn that, in those days before much 'development', a winding road led through the Forest of Arden 23½ miles to this romantic Warwickshire town. There was, however, an argument going on at the moment about the new theatre which was being condemned as 'just like a factory'.

The fields and trees were dim in the cold, but it was a relief to see them after Birmingham's dirty red brick. The road was almost empty, and we sped through the wide street of Henley-in-Arden. The only Henley I had heard of was the one on the Thames. Geo. W. also confused me by continually talking about Broadway. The only Broadway I knew was in New York. I thought he meant that at first, but it did not fit.

The signposts were astonishing. Those historic places which for me before had only been parts of books – Kenilworth, Warwick, Worcester, Malvern – were also near Birmingham. Signposts in an unknown land are always exciting. I was dazzled.

Like everybody seeing a famous place for the first time I was excited yet disappointed at Stratford. It was only an ordinary town after all, with red brick as well as half-timbered houses. But Geo. W., anxious that I should appreciate the Midlands, proposed a visit to the church. Mrs Geo. W., who must have been sated with Stratford trips, said she would stay in the car. There was no difficulty in parking in those days.

We walked in the damp cold along the church's bare lime-tree avenue. The church was closed – which would be odd today for a Sunday afternoon – but the grass was very green and I had glimpses of the brown river. The presence of Geo. W. constrained me and it was very cold, but there was a wonder about this place – Shakespeare's place.

But I was glad to return to the car with its rugs. 'We might just look at the Cotswolds,' Geo. W. said.

Again I could hardly believe my ears. The Cotswolds? I had thought they were in some quite different part of England. Geo. W. drove over an old bridge – Stratford's new bridge had not yet come – and out into the dimming misty afternoon. Presently we were among slopes – grassy or brown and ploughed with a powdering of snow along the furrows. I kept looking for steep heights, for mountain chains, but they were not there; only it seemed ordinary gentle slopes. And the stone houses, which later were to seem so picturesque and ideal, appeared brown and flat like cardboard.

'Perhaps we had better turn back,' Geo. W. said presently with the sky darkening, and I was glad. So we returned, sweeping along the wintry empty roads, and climbed out as stiff as pokers. A glowing fire and toast warmed us a little, and then Geo. W. and I had to go into town for Sunday work.

This was the first of a series of visits I made to homes of members of the staff. I suppose they had been told to entertain me. I met wives and a sister who volunteered comic amused confidences about their menfolk, and talked, as usual, about their children and education. I must have been very naive because I held forth about fishing, saying that it was cruel, in the home of a man who had a passion for it. Gradually I was to learn that the Midlands, with all the canals, were full of fishermen, who spent their weekends on the banks of the waterways and left behind an ungodly mess of paper and bottles. Gradually, too, I learned to be a little more cautious in expressing opinions.

But I must have become intimate with some of the ladies, for I remember Mrs L.P.H., wife of the phlegmatic assistant editor, showing me a book of poetry that he had given her when they were engaged. It seemed that he had deteriorated; had become just a pipe-smoking leader writer going in to the same office year in, year out. But I did remember that in his office room he had a large repro-duction of Hobbema's 'Avenue' which, with its Dutch space and distance, gave a sense of wider horizons than those of Birmingham politics. In the L.P.H. home itself I liked the books and forgot that he was a fisherman.

The visits to the editorial staff tailed off, but Mrs L.P.H., who was a member of several charity committees – and had already suggested Mayfield as a respectable haven for me – had an influence on my future. She had heard that I was interested in social work, and advised me to go and see the wardens of the Birmingham Settlement.

Summer Lane

On that first evening when I was exploring Birmingham I had gone down a hill next to a station – which turned out to be the city's Snow Hill – past black arches to a region of cobbles, huddled poor little shops, great chimneys and dim lighting. Now, when I went to call on the Birmingham Settlement, I saw it all again, but in damp afternoon light when Summer Lane, in spite of its name, looked inexpressibly dreary. You turned right from the shabby main road and found a stretch of cobbles and a gasworks. The road narrowed and went on finally to a vista of tall chimneys.

This was one of the worst areas in the sordid ring of decayed small brick properties round the centre of Birmingham. I spoke at first of Summer Lane as a 'slum', but the residents naturally resented that, though they did admit that it was more difficult to get a job if you lived in the Lane. I was struck later by the fact that the professional people in comfortable Edgbaston and Harborne knew very little of the back streets. Some of the great Birmingham families, led by the Cadburys, were extremely charitable, giving money and premises for schools and children's homes. But they had little personal contact with the dwellers in the Summer Lane areas. There might have been two Birminghams.

Summer Lane went a little uphill and on for a long way. Small side roads came in at right angles, and at many of the corners were pubs. Bordering the Lane were low dirty brick fronts, with brick arches leading into darkness. They were the ways into the courts behind, and stood over cellars that were generally damp or flooded. The courts, I was to find later, were irregularly-shaped wastes of grey sets with tumble-down buildings round and sometimes a tap in the centre. The buildings were chiefly half houses, the other half facing on to the street or another court. Each half house – generally with a door ajar because the windows would not open – consisted of a kitchen which might have a sink or might not, a winding staircase leading up to one bedroom and an attic above. In the kitchen, sometimes with strings of washing above and a slopped wooden table in the middle and with a Victorian range for cooking and heating, lived families which might run to eight or nine members. Other buildings in the courts included a communal lavatory, often out of order, and the 'brew-us' where some kind of drink used to be brewed but where now washing was done. It held an old sink, and the concrete floor was generally full of puddles.

Here and there in Summer Lane were small shabby shops, selling hot food including 'faggot and peas', small groceries, sweets, cigarettes and newspapers. One of the better shops I was to visit later sold garments – cheap blouses, cotton underclothes, babies' outfits and small draperies. In the stretch of the Lane which I was to know later was also a junk shop selling odds and ends of furniture and metal objects.

Summer Lane was developed, I was told, at a time when workers were pouring into Birmingham factories and had to have somewhere to live. For their time, which must have been about the middle of the last century, the houses were considered good and solid. And in one way the arrangement of dwellings in courts was sensible. Dirty and ugly as they were, the courts gave space for the children to play and women to shout across from their doorways. Quarrels went on but also much neighbourly friendliness. And here and there a doorway or window might have a few spindly plants, or there might be a small patch with a scraggy elder bush. To me these were like oases in deserts.

But there was not a tree to be seen in the Lane except for spindly hawthorns and privets in front of the Settlement. The only official open space where children could play was a small grim paved 'rec' in a side street. Once I asked a council official if it could not be grassed over like other recreation grounds to provide a bit of green. 'How long do you think the grass would last?' he asked.

The Settlement, I found, stood high above the road, with a few tangled bushes and sweep of gravel in front of it. It was an old roomy creaking house with steps in front, and a large hall had been built on behind. It was part of that movement which began in London last century for educated men to live among the poor and share their lives. The large provincial cities followed London's example and began their own settlements.

When I called at the Birmingham Settlement it was unusual in having two wardens, inseparable friends. It was also occupied by social-work students taking a two-year course at Birmingham University and one or two academic women who needed a temporary refuge. One in my time was a German refugee, for Birmingham, with its numerous Quakers, was beginning to help Jewish people to leave Hitler's Reich. The Settlement ran clubs, including one for mothers in the afternoon and others for children in the evening. A nursery school occupied the hall during the day, and in the few hot summer weeks the children could be seen having their afternoon rest on the open space in front of the building.

I climbed the bare creaking stairs to the wardens' office, and was received graciously. Mrs L.P.H. had mentioned me. There was a difficulty because I was working in the evening when most of the activities took place, but I could take on a 'provident' round – an effort to get the people of the courts to save. Collectors were given districts and went round with bags for the coins and books to record the savings which were generally a penny or twopence a week. Each saver had a printed card on which the weekly savings were entered. People could have their money out at a week's notice. The sums were too small for them to receive any interest, but the few shillings they saved over the weeks were useful for special needs – a new pair of shoes, the August holiday week when they got no wages, or even a funeral.

I agreed to come each Tuesday afternoon to cover a small part of the Lane and side streets. So began a contact with the courts that was to last fifteen years and to continue, with some faithful friends, after I had left Birmingham.

Reporting

'I think you might go and see Miss Lloyd,' Geo. W. said soon after I arrived. It had been understood that I should do some reporting on women's affairs.

Miss Lloyd, he said, was a member of a well-known Birmingham family. She had been a member of the Council and was known for her public services. Now that she was eighty, and her birthday was being celebrated it would be a good idea for me to go and have a talk with her.

The Daily would make all the arrangements and find out when I could call. I was told that Miss Lloyd would be pleased to see me, but I started out with some nervousness. I had never conducted an interview before and I was so new to reporting that I did not even take a notebook with me. Also I had the disadvantage of looking younger than my years. Several times already I had been met with the comment, 'Why, you're only a child.'

Miss Lloyd lived in an affluent road in Edgbaston where there were ample houses built for large families and front gardens flanked with trees. When I knocked, a neat maid came to the door and led me into an immense room with a cheerful fire.

And now I had to revise one of the prejudices instilled by Cambridge. It had been assumed that wealthy families in manufacturing and commerce were quite uncultivated in art and literature. But I was beginning to find that the large trading families in Birmingham – particularly the women – were highly intelligent and cultivated. I was to hear later that the favourite book of Mrs Neville Chamberlain, wife of the future Prime Minister, was *The Golden Bough* by Sir James Fraser – the massive anti-Christian survey of ancient customs which for us at Cambridge had symbolised freedom from religion.

The walls of Miss Lloyd's big room were covered with small paintings, mainly landscapes and portraits as far as I remember, and there were shelves of books, large armchairs and a soft carpet. It was altogether a cultivated lavish room.

Then Miss Lloyd came in. She was a little deaf, but there was no difficulty in getting her to talk. She poured out details about her large family and her memories, and I had no need to prod her with questions. Afterwards I went straight to the office and wrote down what I remembered, and Geo. W. told me afterwards that Miss Lloyd had written a letter of thanks. She did not know how new I was to the job.

Other small reporting tasks were not as successful. Arriving in this unfamiliar city I knew nothing of local traditions or susceptibilities, nor did I consider them important. I wrote notices in those early days which made me blush afterwards. I was sent to King Edward's

High School for Girls, the best-known girls' school in Birmingham, to report on a Shakespeare production, and one of the actors told me afterwards that they were amazed at the harsh things I said about them.

They bore it in silence, but one girls' school at Edgbaston did not. I had been told by a resident at Mayfield that the school did better in the arts than in academic subjects. I incorporated this judgment into my notice, and the headmistress wrote in protest. Geo. W. came to me in his usual mild way.

'Be careful what you say. You may be perfectly right about the school – I am sure you are – but remember that a local paper can't make sweeping judgments as the nationals can. Our readers are on our doorstep.'

This rebuke filled me with gloom. I was always afraid of doing something which would get me the sack. But shortly afterwards I met the Daily's music critic in New Street. He was gloomy too. 'No real criticism,' he said, 'is possible on a provincial paper. You write a sharp notice on a singer, and next morning meet her in the street.'

In those early days Geo. W. gave me a less personal job. Had I heard of the British Industries Fair, the great annual exhibition to call attention to British achievement? It was held in the late winter in two places. London had the decorative lighter side, and Castle Bromwich, the Birmingham outer suburb, the heavy industries. The London Letter ladies did descriptive paragraphs about the London end. Would I go to the Castle Bromwich end and find something of interest to women?

'Mr Cole is going,' Geo. W. said.

Mr Cole was the senior of the Daily groups two photographers, an amiable stocky man with whom I was later to make many journeys. He was waiting for me outside the office in his small car on a biting February morning. It was the press day, the day before the fair opened to the public. We went through unknown dreary streets till we reached a more open district, and there was a vast hall – freezing cold and vaporous, with here and there the glow of a small brazier as those unpacking the great crates tried to keep warm. With the packing cases, huge piles of straw and paper, towering machines and concrete floor, the place was non-human, colourless and above all cold. Where were women's interests?

George Cole and I separated. He knew his job. He had taken photographs at Castle Bromwich before. I wandered among the machine monsters looking for goods that might relate to women – if possible from Midland firms. There was not much – mainly saucepans and kitchen ware. The 'thirties were a period that liked bright and mixed colours, and coloured kitchen and bathroom ware was coming in. Instead of the standard cream enamels you could have blues and greens and pinks, with walls of the same colour. All the goods that I saw were enamelled metal or ceramics. Plastics had not yet taken over in the kitchen.

I was given a luxurious press lunch at Castle Bromwich. For the first time I discovered how reporters are wooed with food and drink and sometimes gifts. Was it dishonest? Everybody else was determinedly eating and drinking. Long afterwards in London the organiser of a glass exhibition told me he was 'laying on plenty of drink or we shan't get any press notices'. In the end, of course, reporters, like the West Bromwich crowd, get used to such entertainment and think it is their due.

I was to go out year after year to Castle Bromwich, and the task grew easier because some of the firms' representatives got to know me. But there was always this glacial cold.

A job that came as a by-product and introduced some odd subjects to the women's page concerned the Soroptimists. This American women's society, equivalent to the Rotarians, had just reached Birmingham, and membership, which consisted of only one representative of each profession, was being built up. As I worked for Birmingham's major paper I was invited to be the journalist member, which was in a way stupid since the city had a few efficient women, older and more experienced, working for papers. However, a certain amount of subtlety and laxness was shown in the choice of members. Another journalist came in as a fashion writer and another as an editor. Similarly, at least two teachers were admitted – a headmistress and a gym mistress from the same school.

The Soroptimists used to have regular luncheon meetings at a Birmingham café. The lunch cost 2s. 9d. which I considered expensive. But, as with the Rotarians, there was generally some speaker afterwards. The speakers dealt with all sorts of subjects, some of which, such as social work, were suitable for a women's page but some of which were not. Never mind. They would all fill up gaps. So I would launch into half-columns on running a paper factory or the electricity supply. One talk I still remember because it was so ecstatic came from the headmistress member, who was much respected. She had been to Iceland for a summer holiday – a very unusual trip in those days – and everything there seemed to be 'delphinium blue'. It was before the days when delphiniums could be red and pink.

The Soroptimist meetings advanced me in the job of reporting. I was in the habit of listening, going on my Summer Lane round and then writing my report of the lecture. But the afternoon gap led to a weakening of memory, and one day I could not remember a date. I had to telephone to various people to get it, and then the brilliant idea struck me that this would not have been necessary if I had had a notebook. I knew hardly any shorthand, having abandoned it in boredom, but I could take notes with my own abbreviations almost as fast as the shorthand writers. Of course I could not always read my writing afterwards, but then they often could not read their shorthand either.

Notebooks have several benefits. They give you something to do with your hands while you are listening, and they make you look important – real newspaper representatives. Like other reporters, however, I kept my book screened from prying eyes. It always had a wild tangle of scribble.

Presently Geo. W. seldom asked me to report events. For I myself enjoyed writing and I always needed women's page material. So I found subjects of my own and wrote pieces in the evening's spare time. Another woman journalist and I agreed that life has extra spice when you use your experiences as 'copy'. I also enjoyed diving into history, and Birmingham had a mass of Victorian records. By the time I left the city fifteen years later I knew the history of nearly every local organisation and of the principal buildings. And when you know a great deal about a place you grow fond of it.

Daughter of Birmingham

One day I received a note from an unknown woman saying that Mrs L.P.H. had mentioned me, and would I have coffee with some friends at the Three Counties Club? The club, in a street off Corporation Street, was considered very aristocratic and was patronised by leading Birmingham ladies. Mr L.P.H. told me in the evening that it was in my interests to accept the invitation as the hostess and her friends were 'influential'. I was growing used to embarrassing meetings. I put on my best coat and hat and arrived punctually at eleven on a raw day. I was shown into a room with a soft carpet and a large fire, round which sat four middle-aged ladies in armchairs. I had an impression of furs, ample garments and finely waved hair. They rose to greet me, and I felt as if I were in the presence of court ladies. They said as usual, 'Oh, but you're such a child.'

It was rather like an official interview in which you know you are making a poor impression. The armchairs were comfortable, the room was warm, and we had creamy coffee and chocolate biscuits. They talked to me pleasantly about Birmingham, saying I ought to see this and that. But they were all acquaintances of one another and would drift off into their own topics. However they did their best.

'You must come and play tennis with my daughter when the weather is warmer,' said one. 'We have a good stretch of garden with a court.'

'You must come to tea,' said another.

'I'll write and fix a date,' said a third.

Then they paused, and I realised that it was time for me to go. I got up and they rose again. As I went out I was aware of their settling back to talk among themselves.

After all, only one of them wrote to me. She invited me to tea, and when I saw her again she was not the one I expected but the women I had noticed least. But she turned out to represent for me all that seemed best in Birmingham. I was to know her for more than fifteen years till she died, suddenly, in her sleep.

She had thin pure white short hair and a thin face with a wide mouth. She was altogether very thin, and her voice had a hoarse undertone, as she had suffered from some mild form of tuberculosis in her youth. Her parents had died young, and she had been brought up by her grandparents. It was a family, Unitarian in religion like so many of the more intelligent Birmingham families, with a strong tradition of civic service. Her old aunt, whom now she visited almost daily, had been a lady mayoress of Birmingham. Like other highly intelligent Birmingham families, this one owned a factory. It was run in a personal way-with the work, people called by their Christian names.

Mrs A. had once had charge of their welfare. This had turned her into an early advocate of birth control. 'I saw how the women's lives were being poisoned by fear of pregnancies,' she said.

When I knew her she was helping at a private birth-control clinic in a back street. Birmingham's Medical Officer of Health was a Roman Catholic, and the official policy was not to give any advice on family planning. Ignoring this, some of the independent women, including doctors, ran the voluntary centre. Mrs A. acted as receptionist.

She was a woman of cool judgment. She said to me once that churchgoing in her youth and little to do with holiness. 'It was a parade to show off your new clothes,' she said. But she had had a problem which caused emotional heart searching in many of the feminists of her generation. Her family was involved in the Suffragette movement, but there were two groups – the militants and those who wanted to get the vote by peaceful means. Unlike some members of her family she would not become a militant.

The Suffragettes, she told me, were strong in Birmingham. Some of those respectable large Edgbaston houses had had their secrets. This was after the hated 'cat and mouse' regulation which allowed prisons to release Suffragettes when they were ill and re-arrest them when they got better. Some of the former prisoners had been hidden for months in those prosperous homes.

Mrs A.'s marriage was unconventional. She loved music and told me once of the happiness of spring evenings early in the century when people put on new dresses and went down to the Midland Institute for concerts. It was possibly there that she met her Frank who also loved music but came of an undistinguished family. I saw him once or twice – a small man of no particular charm and with a Birmingham voice but genial. Presumably she might have married into one of the prosperous city clans. Instead she had a red brick house in a side street. She said very little about herself, but the marriage was apparently happy.

She had other difficult choices to make. After her early lung trouble she was 'delicate' and her two boy babies were born dead. The doctor told her that she would risk her life if she tried again, but she wanted children and she risked it. A daughter was born and survived. Oddly, though, the girl turned out to be quite different from her parents. She did not like music, and at school was known for her shyness and silence. Mrs A. was gently amused at her, but they were probably alike in some things. When I first met Winifred she was going round public houses collecting money for charity, and she soon married and had a girl and a boy. Mrs A. was an affectionate grandmother. I remember going to Winifred's house and the little girl running out and clasping Mrs A. round the knees. But she did not talk of them much. She preferred to converse on Birmingham history and literature.

It was the same when Frank died. He had a sudden heart attack at night, and she was alone with him. It must have been a shattering experience, but she hardly alluded to it when I next called. It was simply not her habit to talk of personal things.

But then she made another independent decision. She said she had always hated housework and wanted to be free of it. So she sold her house and went to live at a club, mainly for nurses, near by in the Hagley Road. When next I saw her she had a single room with only an electric kettle to provide tea. If she had not been the same Mrs A. one might have felt that she was diminished. At it was we discussed Tolstoi and she borrowed my *War and Peace* which she said she had never read.

After a year or so, however, she began to feel the need for a place of her own, and she bought a primitive cottage, miles from anywhere, in Worcestershire. Here she entertained her family and friends at weekends. When I visited her she showed me a sweet-briar hedge with its scented leaves that she had planted. 'I've always wanted a briar hedge,' she said. I had not seen this love of flowers before.

In Birmingham she was on the committee of the old Margaret Street Library, founded as a private venture in the eighteenth century and still combining a private club and library in its dignified Victorian building. In the committee room was a long table and here newly published books were laid out. The committee came in through the week to examine them, and on Fridays met to vote on which they would take.

Later I was a committee member briefly but never had time to spend long over the books. Mrs A. conscientiously spent hours looking them through. She was amused at some of the prejudices of other members. For some reason they detested the Sitwells who had a reputation for brilliance at the time. Perhaps the Yorkshire family's aristocratic posing annoyed the solid Birmingham citizens.

Long afterwards in London I met a university librarian who had been with Mrs A. on the committee. She was the one he remembered. 'Yes. She was a very nice woman,' he said.

Mrs A.'s nursing club was bombed in the war, but she did not complain. She was mainly interested in the curious effects of the explosion – an aspect of the raids which we had not foreseen. The bomb fell in front of the building, but the trees and the front were hardly damaged. At the back, however, most of the windows were broken.

But while most people were talking excitely of raids and fearful nights she remained almost detached. I met her one day outside the Town Hall when raids were at their height and she began to talk to me of *Roderick Hudson*, Henry James's early novel. Did I agree that it was one of his best?

Mrs A. would never tell anybody her age because, she said, she had a horror of having her arm taken and being led across the road. But we could have worked it out if we had liked because she went almost daily to see her old aunt who was eighteen years older and complained of the burden of age. Old Mrs B. 'Auntie, and Mrs A. had been brought up together, but the old lady was far wilder and more eccentric. Her house, a large imposing dwelling, and the maid in a white frilled apron who opened the door, hinted at a wealthy background, and Mrs B. had once been Lady Mayoress of Birmingham. But she was a tiny wispy woman with her hair drawn back in a bun, a small soft hand, a soft way of speaking and a wicked gleam in her eye. She made wild statements with a twinkling sideways glance, and declared that she was an atheist and her favourite author was George Moore who had undermined the Gospels with his novel *The Brook Kerith*. Now and then when she made some flighty statement Mrs A. would laugh and say, 'She doesn't mean it.'

Auntie was over eighty and suffering from old age. She could not sleep, she said, and spent the night playing patience. My last memory of her was of her farewell on her imposing doorstep. She put her soft tiny hand in mine and said, 'I've had enough, my dear. I want to go' She did go soon afterwards.

Mrs A. herself lived till after I had left Birmingham. She continued to entertain me and others of my generation and talk of books and the past in the city. While she gave us comfortable teas she always said, 'It's so good of you young people to visit me.' I must have heard that remark a dozen times, while in reality we were the ones who were benefiting. When later I heard that she had been found dead in bed I was, as one always is, incredulous.

While Birmingham had a number of exotics she represented to me all that was best in the local well-to-do families, with their liberalism, energy and freedom of thought. Her favourite word, I remember, was 'integrity'.

Parties and Journeys

Articles, typed but corrected in very black ink in a sprawling hand, presently began to arrive from an O.A.M.-H. They were on exotic places, and I thought for a time that they were by a man. Then the author rang up and turned out to be a woman.

Presently O.A.M.-H., who liked to be called 'Onera', asked me to visit her. She lived, uncharacteristically, in a roomy red Victorian house in Harborne, but the large garden suited her since she was an ardent gardener growing all sorts of foreign and unusual plants.

She was an American, middle-aged, plump, curly-haired and formidable with blunt features, a curling lip and a habit of shocking people. She had come from one of the southern States but had married a Birmingham dentist and then been divorced. Now she took vast journeys alone and was writing a book on Mexico. She wandered round Iran, then called Persia, which was so unusual a journey that local people were not impressed because they thought she had been to the Worcestershire town of Pershore.

I remember her saying when she returned from Mexico that lavatories had been her chief difficulty, and it was a pity that man had natural functions. She also talked a great deal about sex, and told a story of how on one boat both a father and a son had proposed to her. But she was also interested in world and especially American politics, and would earnestly ask her guests' opinions on the president or New York publications which they knew little about.

Soon I was visiting her regularly, always picking up new information. She had American papers about and seemed to have correspondents, chiefly men, in many places. I heard a little of her background. She had three children, one of whom had settled in South Africa. When this one was a baby, Mrs M.-H. had taken some examination at Birmingham University and brought the child with her in a carrycot. This had remained beside her as she wrote.

Now she had frequent visitors, but was not a conventional hostess. She asked the young men to empty their own chamber-pots in the morning, and sometimes she would retire to her room and leave them to their own devices. She loved shocking people and described to me, because she knew that I was a vegetarian, the buckets of blood she got from the local butcher to feed her vine. She was an excellent cook, preparing all sorts of exotic dishes. But her kitchen was a wild dusty muddle.

She had the walls of her drawing-room painted black, and here she held eighteenth-century salons. A group of about a dozen guests would assemble and be served with exotic cigarettes, sweetmeats and Turkish coffee. They would sit in a large circle and discuss sex, politics, religion, topics of the day. Mrs M.-H. was clever at capturing well-known people. At her salons I met Naomi Mitchison, the novelist, Helen Gardner, the literary critic, and other figures from

Birmingham University. On Saturday evenings guests often stayed so late that the buses had finished and those without cars had to walk home.

Many people must have been stimulated by Mrs M.-H. But because of her odd manners and sex talk Birmingham ladies looked on her with some reserve. I certainly did not show enough gratitude.

Not only did she entertain me but she took me, generally with one of her sons, on long motoring journeys, often at peculiar times. From her old car I had a November view of the desolate wastes bordering the 'new' Wolverhampton road – the broken rusty fragments of iron, the spurts of coarse grass, the shacks and gaunt black chimneys along the horizon. In the old days, I was told, you could see the chimneys flaring against the night sky, but the depression had quenched most of them.

We went on to the Wrekin – the highest hill in Britain because it is not quite a thousand feet tall and so is not a mountain – on a dripping misty day. There was nobody about, but we toiled round and round up muddy paths with wet yellow leaves above. We attempted the Cotswolds in the deep snow, and the car stuck on a bank and had to be pushed off. It must have been winter when we climbed above the Elan Valley from which Birmingham got its water supply – one of the great engineering feats on which the city plumed itself. It was beginning to get dark, water gleamed below; the dim mountains were round us, and there was a sense of peace after Birmingham brick. But we had to turn back as I had to begin work at 6.30 on a Sunday evening.

At this time London Zoological Society opened its estate at Whipsnade, and Mrs M.-H. determined to visit it. We got up at about five o'clock as far as I remember, and raced south – without, of course, the M1. It was a huge journey, but Whipsnade was a disappointment, for only a few animals had so far been installed and they were mainly invisible in their large paddocks.

One of the most exquisite spring sights I ever had came from Mrs M.-H. She was staying in a cottage at Harlech in April, and I went there for the weekend. To return to Birmingham on the Monday morning I had to travel south to Barmouth along the coast, and I caught a slow local train crawling along by a blue sea. I stood at the window gazing. I had never seen such flowers – gorse, primroses, violets, blackthorn and others – brilliant on a sunny morning. Finally we had blue water on both sides as we crossed the estuary, and I was almost glad. You cannot sing hymns at heaven's gate for very long at a time.

Mrs M.-H. moved out of Birmingham when the war came, but I still visited her in the country. She lived alone – she did not like pets – with a gun to protect her from marauding men or animals. She still seemed to be getting many American papers and she still cooked exotic dishes and discoursed on sex. She was probably much older than she appeared. We never knew. She died a few years after the war.

There were other exotics in Birmingham in the 'thirties. One claimed to be a Russian princess and had the noted name of Trubetskoy. Another White Russian, living in Shropshire, was an authority on mediaeval books and handwriting. She could decipher monks' Latin and recognise the different handwriting of different centres of learning. She had all this scholarship, but she could not make a living with it. She brought out one small book, and I wanted her to continue. But no. The public did not want learning. So she began to write sentimental books about well-known people, such as Catherine the Great, with a Russian background and made money and a reputation.

Contributions

The rubbish that had poured in after the Daily's first advertisements gradually died down, but still people who had never seen the women's page continued to send in impossible effusions. Still I was assailed with verse – pious popular rhymes such as 'Give a smile. It's always worthwhile', or verse imitating Walter de la Mare who was popular at the time, or imitating T. S. Eliot who was popular with university students.

Then of course hundreds of household hints came in. They were often long and complicated directions, founded on Mrs Beaton and the Victorians, for making a polish or cleaner that could now be bought for a few pence in the shops. Or there were involved suggestions for removing wine stains. These household hints differed from those of today which stress the new inventions and their up-to-dateness. These delighted in the past and asserted that 'Grandmamma knew best'.

I had Grandmamma's instructions for making wines and pot-pourri. 'Old time' and 'well-tried' were favourite words. Flower arrangement as a hobby had not yet come in, but at Christmas and

Easter time-wasting crafts flourished. You could dye poppy heads and grass, dry flowers and scatter artificial frost over everything. You could preserve roses, which then had a much shorter flowering season, by dipping their cut stems in glycerine, wrapping them in tissue paper and putting them away in a drawer. Easter, of course, was the time for dying eggs, with notes on the Easter habits of the Russians – not the shocking Stalin gang but the simple peasants whose virtues, like Grandmamma's cookery, lingered from the past. I also had photographs and articles on bulb-planting in pots – not an expensive hobby, as hyacinth bulbs cost threepence each and daffodils a penny.

Some of the household hints had the nauseating habit, not yet fully dead, of turning furnishings into people: 'Your curtains will love a bath of fluffy soap-suds' or 'Make your floors smile at you with this fine cleaner.' Little of such stuff was kept, and in any case you could boil down two pages of this sort of thing into two paragraphs.

Another genre which I detested was a trick story – made popular, probably, by the American writer O'Henry. It might be a story about the wayward and beautiful Clementine with her long dark hair. She is the light of the household, but one day she leaves without a word. Agonising enquiries ensue, but there is no trace. Then a blood-curdling shriek rings out. There has been a murder in the garden. Agony on agony till Clementine, the family cat, walks in. Of course one had guessed the catch long before.

Men wrote satiric sketches about 'the wife' who was then a 'little woman'. She was extravagant and brainless, but she had endearing ways. She cooked an elaborate supper – probably with chicken which was more of a luxury then – and after the meal perched on her husband's knee, stroked his hair and asked for money for a new hat. She did not have money of her own, of course. She was middle-class; she did not work.

Meanwhile the home-bound wives wrote about their servants and charwomen. The working-class woman, in spite of many children, had always laboured for her betters. She was one of the links for her mistress with another world. The charwomen of the articles had extravagant habits, ate the wrong food, were in debt, dropped their Hs, and were generally comic. Or sometimes they could be pathetic if they were old or had bad legs or sick children.

As the great age of air travel had not arrived and much of Europe was untouched by tourism, I had an abundance of travel articles about little – or even well – known places. Birmingham families at this date went to Bournemouth, Devon or Wales for polite holidays or to Blackpool or Llandudno for holidays with fun. But professional people, many of them women teachers, would spend a fortnight in Innsbruck or Verona and earn travel money by writing about them afterwards. They did not touch politics but dwelt on the scenery and the warm hearts of the natives.

History was useful. It was an important subject in the schools, and the public was interested in the past – particularly the past of their own localities. When I had lived in the south I had thought of British history – except for a few battles and forays against the Welsh and Scots – as being concentrated on London, but now Birmingham, calling itself the Midland capital and resenting London dominance, also proved to have a stirring past – from Prince Rupert's attack in the Civil Wars onward. It was new territory – the eighteenth-century giants such as Baskerville the printer Boulton, Watt and Priestley, and then the great charitable and reforming figures of the nineteenth century, with Cardinal Newman at the Oratory. The Chamberlains were still living figures.

As for the Midlands, they were bristling with history – from Warwick and Kenilworth Castles to Boscobel Oak. I took most of the historical articles that came in. They were of course a minority, but now and then I got a bit of original research. A man, probably elderly, who sent in scrawling uneducated writing on thin pages, was an authority on the eighteenth-century theatre in the provinces. He knew about the tours of the various companies and the theatre buildings appearing in the provincial towns. It was something I had never thought of before.

A Hampstead woman began to send articles on Le Corbusier and new styles in architecture with their concrete and flat roofs. I don't think Geo. W. knew much about Le Corbusier, but he was tolerant and interfered little. The architecture articles were untidily corrected as by an intellectual woman not interested in neatness, but they were useful as they were accompanied by photographs which filled in gaps when others pictures were scarce. What Birmingham readers, used to the terracotta ornamentation and pinnacles of the city, thought of these stark buildings I did not hear. They would probably have preferred the mock-Tudor villas that were springing up in ribbon development along the main roads.

Correspondence of many types in all sizes of envelopes was waiting in my solid wooden tray each evening. From time to time I had scrawls from a madman. Crooked Scripture messages of doom covered the envelopes, and inside were jumbles of end-of-the-world prophecies culled mainly from the Book of Revelation. The madman never put in his address; so I could not send them back. They went into a drawer and got very dusty.

The articles that were accepted were published in long columns with small headlines, lengthy paragraphs and a few cross headings. They were signed only by initials or, if they were general reports, not at all. We had to avoid advertising and often got into difficulties over trade names. We wrote of 'sixpenny stores' – Woolworth's in those days sold nothing over sixpence – or a 'well-known saloon car'. Some names – 'thermos' for example – turned out to be trade names when I did not know it.

Lavatory and sex matters we did not mention. There was no awkward restraint about this. Nobody mentioned them in reputable papers except, I suppose, medical publications. I knew nothing of four-letter words and when, later on, I used to have obscene telephone calls at two a.m., and the caller pressed me to repeat a certain term, I told him in a school-mistressy way that there was no such word in the English language.

In the Office

I used to get a good many visitors in my room in the early evening One was R.C.R., the Daily's dramatic critic, who had some reputation beyond Birmingham. He had a round smiling face, a dimpled chin and white hair though he was only in his forties. He had been educated at the local King Edward's High School, and had made a name by researches on local history and the theatre. He was one of a group involved in the building of the new theatre at Stratford which was being bitterly attacked for looking like a factory, with its flat roof and simple lines.

Office gossip said he was living a merry life and had married a barmaid. He liked talking to girls and would drift in smiling and hold forth about his researches at Stratford. He said that there was no evidence that Shakespeare was born in the Birthplace except that his father was prosecuted for having a muck heap in the street. There was more than one Anne Hathaway, and the famous cottage probably belonged to the wrong one.

He would stand urbanely chatting for a few minutes and then

drift out, cheerfully greeting somebody outside the door. Everybody liked him. 'Garn,' he would say. Once, when I had my first old car he suggested I should motor him to Stratford, and he would show me the theatre.

The trip was spoiled for me by two things. I was always afraid that the car would break down, and R.C.R. knew nothing of cars either. Suppose it broke down, or suppose I parked it and then could not find it? Luckily – and it was always luck rather than judgment with me – I got it back safely. The other flaw was that R.C.R. stayed gossiping with acquaintances at the back of the theatre while the play, which I think was 'Lear', was proceeding. I suppose he knew Shakespeare too well to bother to listen, but I was sick to stand there in all the cigarette smoke and hear only a faint voice intoning in the distance.

But beforehand I had been shown all the modern wonders of the stage – the way the curtains were controlled, the lifting and scenery-moving devices, the revolving mechanism. In the 'thirties the stage machinery was regarded as the most modern in Europe.

Then suddenly R.C.R. died of pneumonia. His was the first of many deaths I was to encounter in that cheerful office. People said he had undermined his health with too much drinking. Perhaps he had. He was a jester and a law to himself, but he made life more amusing. He left no children.

Ned, the handsome stooping chief reporter with a room next to mine, had a mixed group of men under him. His deputy was a gentle man with a stammer who suffered from epileptic fits. It was a sign of the benevolence of the office that a man so afflicted could rise to such a position. One evening I was told that he had had a seizure and had fallen down, but the reporters had known what to do and had put a pencil between his teeth to stop his biting his tongue, and when he came to himself had taken him home. He would be back in a day or two, they said.

The reporters themselves were a mixed lot. The older ones had left school at fourteen and worked their way up. They wrote their pieces instead of typing them and were full of clichés – 'a good time was had by all', 'the festive season', 'the cup that cheers'. The younger ones typed their work, were better educated and more ambitious.

They too gossiped. One older man told me that the worst job he ever had was to call at a Birmingham bishop's house when he was dying and ask for bulletins – an illustration of the Daily's old-fashioned methods and avoidance of horror-reporting. One dapper reporter, always dressed well in a dark suit, was a local preacher – hardly what one would have expected. The sports editor was also a pious pillar of his chapel. Another reporter, a Welshman, was known as a humorist, and tales were told of his repartee. The reporters used to bring weekly claims for expenses to be signed, and in the past 'Joe' Gorman, now literary editor, had dealt with them. Once Dai laid his account before Joe and Mr Gorman took up his eyeglass to study it. Dai said, 'You needn't magnify it, Mr G. I've magnified it enough already.'

There were also friendly characters among the sub-editors who sat in their enclosed room dealing with the news. The reserved urbane chief sub-editor with his glass eye told me that he still had memories of trench warfare and dreamed of leaping over a parapet and bayoneting a German. The war had cast its shadow on a number of the Daily men. It had also, of course, been a break from workaday lives and a widening of experience and they liked to tell stories of it.

The deputy chief sub-editor, sitting in the front row and sometimes taking the presiding place facing the others, was another George and seemed too kind to be true. He was the one with bright brown eyes, hair that was early white and hands that he could turn to anything. He got into the habit of doing jobs for me – putting my typewriter right, procuring me sharp scissors, looking up addresses. I probably took these attentions too much for granted. He told me that the only thing wrong about his marriage was that it had not come early enough. He loved his two children, always speaking with emotional softness about the 'wonderful kid', his daughter. He died quite young after the second war had scattered us.

But the greatest concentration of amusing characters was 'upstairs' in the composing room. Mick, the sturdy, black-haired Communist, was a general joke for his politics. He would argue about the glories of Russia though he had never been there, while his companions laughed and made sly jokes. There were gentle family men and a man looking like a broad-backed Indian colonel who was at the desk and gave out copy to the machine men. A little bright-eyed apprentice, Dick, was serving his seven years, and a man whom I called 'Big Boy', who sometimes made up my page, was tall and like a Greek god, with a fluff of fine gold hairs along his arms. But he was rather dumb, and it was difficult to strike a spark out of him. One of the men in the photographic department was a spastic with a flapping head and speech difficult to understand – another example of the firm's kind employment policy. The men, except for Wag and his small amiable deputy, wore white aprons which got smeared with ink and streaked when they wiped their sweaty hands.

Wag himself towered among the printers who were mainly small men. He was alarmingly efficient, shouting and working like a madman in a crisis, but generally our relationship was genial. When he came down to see me each evening he might stop a minute or two to retail office gossip. Sometimes I would go up to consult him in the peaceful pause while the printers were in the canteen at supper. The lights would be turned down in the warm composing room, and in the half darkness I would find Wag in his box eating his own supper. I would climb the steps and he would bid me stay and drink a cup of weak tea and eat a chocolate biscuit. We would sit on high stools by the wooden shelving and talk a minute or two, and there would be quietness all around with the clacking machines stopped.

Wag made up my page for the first few days, working with great energy, dropping in type and picture blocks with a flourish, striding off to find small items of news to fill the gaps, rapidly reckoning on the cuts needed in articles. He had the page ready well before ten, the time limit. But one evening he said to me, ''Ere, I've got somebody to make up your page,' and there standing behind the silver slab called 'the stone' was a small man with a red face, very blue eyes, light brown hair and half a finger missing.

So began my acquaintance with one of the best men I ever met, who also became one of my closest Birmingham friends. His name was Teddy but for some obscure reason I called him Pimmy. I saw him sometimes nervous and upset at something Wag had said, and I saw him possessed with wild merriment at some joke when he would slap his knee and roar with laughter. But I never saw him bad-tempered or mean in any way. He was easily hurt but unfailingly good-natured, and he got on well with the other printers.

At first he was nervous and over-obliging, but before long we were completely easy. As we worked we talked, and I learnt that his wife, Lil, was not very strong, and he had a boy of eight and an old mother. He lived in a new estate at Yardley, half an hour's bus ride from the centre of the city, and still almost a village with an ancient church with a spire. Several printers lived out there, and the wives, lonely in the evenings, used to visit one another.

Presently Pimmy was asking me out to see his wife and garden. He gave me his garden produce, and later even found me an old car. He also gave me advice which has sometimes served well since. When the page was late and Wag was shouting or there had been some other bother, he always said, 'Take no notice.'

I occasionally unwittingly did him a bad turn. I used to go straight to work after visiting the back courts of Summer Lane. There must have been many fleas about, and I would bring one or two of them back. Pimmy's fair moist skin seemed irresistible to them. 'You gave me one of them things again,' he would say, but he never minded.

Pimmy had lost his half finger in the war, but he hardly seemed to miss it and handled type quite easily. But, as with others in the office, his war-time experiences lingered with him. Sometimes he would say as I finished in the composing room, 'Goodnight Nurse.'

Troubles

'My wife,' Geo. W. said to me gently one day, 'isn't sure that all the recipes on the women's page are quite practical. There was one yesterday about rice . . . I know it's the contributors' fault,' he added generously. 'But . . . my wife says she'll be pleased to look through any recipes you get.'

I must have published some odd cookery instructions in those early days. Recipes were not given much prominence as I hated the usual feminine repertoire, but I did use them to fill corners. I had done plenty of cooking at home, but the trouble was that I was now a vegetarian, and every time meat was mentioned I had visions of the abattoir. So I tended to tinker with what came in. I had always experimented in cooking anyhow.

With a heart like lead and a hatred of Geo. W.'s friendly gossipy wife, I gave him a sheaf of recipes. He came back with them in a few days and said she had approved most of them but discarded a few. Nothing more was said, and she did not ask to see my recipes again. But I was more careful afterwards, not inventing so much. One could always give recipes for cakes and puddings which did not involve meat.

But after some months a more serious trouble suddenly struck. It came from an incredible piece of bad luck. One contributor whom I found better than most was a London woman writing about folklore. She sent untidy scrawled-over typescripts, but she seemed to have done original research. I had used several of her articles, and she must have kept an eye on the page – not an invariable practice with contributors living out of the area.

One day I received an angry letter from her. She said that an article of hers which had appeared in the *Sunday Express* a few weeks before had now been published by 'Women's Interests', word for word the same but over different initials.

The 'thief' was Bernard who had saved me from despair in London and had helped me to get the Birmingham job. He was an expert on antique furniture, and had stayed on the women's magazine where we had met, and was eventually to become its editor. Meanwhile he had regularly sent me articles which I had published. I had thought vaguely, I now realised, that the folklore article came strangely from him, but no conscious query had risen in my mind. But now I wrote to ask for an explanation.

I shall never know the rights of the matter. I had seen how he did not object to a little sharp practice in journalism, but he surely would not have deceived a young protégée for whom he felt affection. Now he threw the blame on his secretary. He said he kept a collection of big envelopes in which he put cuttings which might be of use later. He had sent the secretary the folklore article and told her to keep it in one of the envelopes. Instead she had typed it out and sent it to me.

I had to accept the explanation. I dared not tell Geo. W. and implicate Bernard. I also had a guilty feeling that I should have read Sunday papers and myself seen the article. Letters went to and fro, and Bernard said he would go along to see the lady and pacify her. But he failed. He wrote that she was 'growling like a mad dog' and would not let him in.

Then the lady wrote to Geo. W. and threatened to go to her solicitors. Geo. W. came in to me with the letter and a puzzled frown. I tried to explain, but the affair had been going on for days and I should obviously have consulted him. 'I don't understand who this Bernard is,' he said patiently. 'Have you his letters?'

I had; but they were pretty personal. Bernard had written to me by my Christian name and his usual affection. Another aspect of my guilt occurred to me. Geo. W. would think that I was specially favouring my friends and taking their articles so that they could make money out of the paper.

Geo. W. said quietly, 'You should have told me,' and took the letters away. I sat with a blank mind. I should be sacked of course and have to return home. It would be my second failure. I had been cheating the paper that had bestowed so many benefits.

Then Geo. W. returned. 'It's a bad business,' he said, but without anger. 'I will write to Miss W.' He gave me back the awful letters. 'Of course this Bernard must never write for us again.'

Not a word about sacking. I waited. Surely it must come. But he walked out as if this were the end of the matter.

I did not know what to think. I had a sick headache and sat without working, head on hand.

Geo. W. returned suddenly. 'Aren't you well?'

I muttered something about neuralgia.

'Well, go home early,' he said. 'Don't bother about anything else tonight.'

It seemed incredible. Hardly a word of blame. But I heard later that the old man always stood up for his staff. What he said to the folklorist I never heard, but there was no case against the Daily. I had to write and tell Bernard that I could not take more articles, and the matter ended.

Our contact, however, was broken. I ceased to hear from him. He died, a respected journalist, many years later.

A similar thing, equally incomprehensible, occurred after some years, and again I had met and respected the writer. She was a teacher at a local grammar school; did voluntary social work and visited the local prison. She began to write articles on the social services, and one day sent me a note on the care of the blind. I used it; and again I had bad luck. It had been taken from a new book, and the author – again not a Birmingham woman – must have known my page. She in her turn wrote and threatened legal action, but this time I took the letter to Geo. W.

He wrote to the respectable teacher, and she admitted to having read the new book but said she had quoted only a few sentences from it. Then the angry author sent us the book, and we could see that the teacher had exactly copied out four pages, adding a little at the beginning and end. Perhaps she did not know that this was an offence, but she should have known. She was far older than I was. In any case, why did she dish out other people's work as her own? I never understood it and I did not meet her again. Geo. W. wrote telling her to send no more articles.

In the squabbles and libel actions of today's journalism such crises might hardly be noticed. But in the Midlands away from London at this period we were much more careful of the paper's good name. We had, too, the feeling of being apart from the strident London papers with their huge circulations. It was the sense of being in a sheltered corner that partly kept people on the Daily for so many years.

Moving

One Saturday evening in the first spring Anne invited me to coffee in her room at Mayfield. That was nice, I thought. It reminded me of the old college days.

Gradually I had come to know the residents of the women's club, though not very well as I was out when most of them were in. Anne, with her ash-blonde hair and pale face, was in her late twenties, and nearest among the residents to my age. She was the one who had been ill and was said to be unhappy.

Over her gas fire we began to talk of the Quakers who were so powerful in Birmingham. Anne, who had been brought up among them, accused them of being narrow-minded and set in their ways. How much this had to do with her emotional affairs I did not know, but she said she wanted to get away.

Then she added, 'Well, anyhow, none of us will be here much longer.'

I did not understand what she meant.

'She should have told you when you came,' Anne said.

The elf, she explained, had been running the club for ten years, and had done well out of it. But now the lease was falling in, and the house was in such a state of disrepair that the owner would have to demolish it. The elf had been trying to raise the money for purchase and repair, but a vast sum was needed. 'People,' Anne said, 'have been leaving because of the uncertainty. That was why there was a room for you.'

I felt pleasantly detached. I had made one move – all the way from Surrey. Now I could make a small one. I was not like the governess of the bishop's children who had lived at Mayfield for ten years at a reduced rate and now did not know where to go.

Mayfield's large garden, with its trees and wide spread of lawn, was a soothing place to sit in on spring mornings. A gardener still kept the lawn velvety, but the corner where residents had had their own small gardens was neglected and full of weeds. The elf with her piping voice remained outwardly cheerful, but there were shadows under her eyes. We heard that she could not raise the money, and somebody wanted to build flats on the site. Residents began to drift away. By June they were all making arrangements to leave. They found flats or other landladies. The elf herself was going to live with a brother. The summer sun showed Mayfield's cracks more than ever, and weeds now covered the gravel in front.

I knew where I wanted to live. I went down Summer Lane and saw the wardens of the Settlement. The old house had a room or two for professional women, and I was allowed one of them. The only stipulation was that I should wait a fortnight till their summer holiday was over.

A teacher resident at Mayfield, who had taken a flat in the centre of town, said I could borrow it for a fortnight since she would be away. So one weekend I packed my bags and said goodbye to the elf, who kept a smiling face to the end. All she asked was that I should write in her guest book. Our complimentary remarks must have been a comfort. A few of the residents invited me to go and see them at their new homes, and then I turned my back for a little on comfortable Edgbaston.

It was strange living in that central street with its noisy traffic, especially since I did not get up till ten in the morning. The street was impersonal, a place of movement and noise, and I used to dream of it afterwards. The door of the flats opened straight on to the pavement. But the small block was purpose-built, and when you had shut the door on the street you became totally apart from it. I went up the stairs to my own nest, where the sun in that hot weather seemed more of a presence than the traffic. It was like being in a house on a cliff, secure above the waves. But there was nowhere to go and nothing to look out on except cars. It did not matter, however, since the stay was short.

Mayfield was soon pulled down and flats took its place.

Settlement People

It was still summer when I moved to the bare large room in the old house above Summer Lane. In the warm nights after work I did not take the office coach but walked to the Settlement, going through streets of silent shops and then plunging downwards to the cobbles and dust. On divine soft blue nights, with the moon glinting on the low slate roofs, I tramped along Summer Lane, where bits of crumpled paper looked white in gutters and occasionally a lean cat dashed out from an entry.

The people at the Daily argued that I was foolish to walk about there alone. They assured me that even the police went down there only in couples. But I never saw anything very sinister. The pubs had closed hours before, and the Summer Lane workers went to bed early because they had to go early to their jobs. Only a constable sometimes moved out of the shadows as I came tramping along.

Those were the summer nights when one longed for woods and country smells, for flower scents and honeysuckle in the hedges. Instead there were the tall chimneys, cobbles and almost nothing green. I was there by choice, but the people of the courts had to live in the town desert all their lives.

As quietly as I could I let myself in at the Settlement's heavy door and creaked up the uncarpeted stairs to my uncarpeted bedroom. The floors cracked. Sleep eluded me and noise began early. When the university term started I got to know every morning movement of the students – their rising, descent to breakfast, return to their rooms and then their departure with the slamming of the heavy front door. People seemed to come to that door all the morning. The maids ran to and fro. Somebody sang. The traffic rumbled by. I got up jaded and had a hasty breakfast.

I had gone out there because I had romantic ideas about helping the poor, but I saw little of the Settlement's work because of my evening absence. What I did see of it made me vaguely uneasy. It was assumed in those days, before the arrival of immigrants with other religions, that if you were interested in social work you were a devout church or chapel goer. A church atmosphere seemed to hang over everything. The two wardens were devoted churchgoers. The students had lecturers among the clergy. I was not a daughter of the Church, and I felt out of it.

Instead my main acquaintances at the Settlement were the two maids. I used to take my breakfast tray down to the kitchen in the morning and we would talk at the foot of the stairs, though they would vanish rapidly if anybody in authority appeared.

The two maids contrasted with one another. Ella, with light smooth brown hair and candid blue eyes, was twenty-one and dovelike, demure in her white cap and apron. She was in every way a good girl; everybody liked her, and she was engaged to a good young man.

Zillah was ten years older, stocky, with curly black hair, a grin and a staring glass eye. She told me that her mother had been a gipsy, and she was like a gipsy herself, laughing and quick at repartee. She had three languages. Her ordinary speech was stock Birmingham, with the singsong intonation and Midland vowels. I understood most of it. But sometimes, for a joke, she went into the broadest Black Country speech, of which I understood hardly a word. Finally she showed off her 'lah-di-dah' talk in which she imitated the ladies and gentlemen of the committee that ran the Settlement. Birmingham's upper classes did not know that the squinting black-haired maid who brought in the tea was listening to their polite accents and making a joke of them in the kitchen.

Zillah could, however, be treacherous, and she led me to a secret conflict with the wardens. She had no family, and she was always complaining of being paid such low wages that she could not afford to go away for a holiday. I, happy with my great income of eight pounds a week, asked her if she would like me to arrange a holiday for her. Yes, yes, she was enthusiastic. I had been writing an article on a society that sent poor Birmingham children to the country, and I knew I could get names of country hostesses. Through the society I found a woman who would take Zillah for a week. Zillah herself was pleased, and I said I would pay.

But she did not go on the holiday. When I had arranged everything she suddenly said she could not go. Why? Oh, it was the wardens. She must have mentioned the holiday to them, and they had told her not to go. They thought it would be bad for the Settlement if it was known that the maids were not earning enough to pay for their own holidays.

But it was all very secret. For some unknown reason the wardens said nothing to me, and I was timid and did not broach the subject with them. I argued with Zillah, saying that all the arrangements had been made. But it was no good. The wardens had told her not to go, and I had to cancel everything. For a time I was angry but never had the courage to make an open protest.

Ella married her good young man. I never heard what happened to Zillah.

I made another acquaintance at the Settlement who was to open my eyes to a whole new group in Birmingham – the first of the German refugees. Dr Hellinger had, I think, had some legal job in her country. But she was Jewish and had early seen the coming danger. With the help of the Quakers she had escaped to England, and was now living at the Settlement till she obtained a permit for the United States. She was a cultivated woman who had been a person of some consequence. Now she had lost everything.

I wanted to learn German, and she gave me lessons and talked about literature. She was glad to converse, and from her I learnt that Birmingham already had a network of refugees who knew one another and met in the evenings. They were mainly cultivated people, but they were allowed to take only menial positions. She was considered extremely lucky to be a shop cashier. I wonder now that we did not feel angrier at the way the refugees had been treated by Germany. But in the 'thirties each European country was a law to itself, and, with memories of the First World War still vivid, we were afraid of anything that might provoke bad feelings. The pacifists' dilemma of the 'thirties was beginning. Do you try to right wrongs at the risk of war, or is war the greatest evil to be avoided at all costs? In the end, of course, we were to find that the catastrophe occurred regardless of us and our noble sentiments. The refugees themselves said that we were living in a fool's paradise.

Some of them in the end reached the United States. Others were prevented by the war and were put into internment camps and moved away from the coast in case they were spies. Some of them did well. After Dr Hellinger had gone, a rosy-cheeked girl of seventeen taught me German. She had been training to be a barrister, but had been sent out of Germany early by her father who was a judge. She finally tried her fortune in South Africa, met and married another Jew there and settled with him in Israel and became a university lecturer.

The half dozen students taking a two-year social-work course at the university were near my own age, but I did not see much of them and felt immeasurably older. But there must have been some intimacy for I remember one of them telling me her problems over a love affair. One of their tutors was a young clergyman whom they all much admired. One day, to Rachel's intense surprise, he approached her and asked her to marry him. 'I hadn't the slightest idea that he liked me,' she said. In her astonishment she asked for time to think. What should she do? She accepted him in the end and the marriage was happy.

Could such a situation occur today? Unlikely, I think. Actually, I came across a similar situation with another Birmingham girl – a proposal coming out of the blue. This marriage was also successful, though she died young. Perhaps the more stable marriages of the 'thirties were due to the sober way people conducted their love affairs.

Just once or twice I attended settlement gatherings of Summer

Lane dwellers. One Saturday evening when I was free I went to one of the dances that were held in the hall behind. I expected to help, but there was little to do. Large numbers of teenagers surged into the hall. A student thumped out dance tunes at a piano on the platform, and others brought plates of buns round at half time; but otherwise the company enjoyed itself in its own way.

Girls came in together giggling, and danced with one another. The boys seldom danced but stood round the sides of the hall and read sporting papers, sometimes sticking out a leg to trip a girl up. Then there would be a chorus of guffaws. The younger boys made catcalls, and they all smoked and fell on the buns when they were brought round. I left before the end.

I went to the Settlement expecting it to be home, but in the end I stayed less than a year.

Outside the Settlement

There was certainly a tangle of bushes outside the Settlement, shielding it from the road. But outside that were miles and miles of tumbledown dirty brick, and every week it was a small effort to start on my provident round. Yet I soon came to realise that I was getting more from those Tuesday afternoon visits than I was giving. Voluntary workers generally find this.

Yet the Summer Lane lives were oppressed by poverty, discomfort and ill health. People accepted it, I suppose, because they were all in the same boat and didn't know anything better. Nor had they the education to know how to protest. Some of the older people could not read or write.

Walls were bug-ridden. Cellars often had standing water. Windows would not open. Lavatories, serving perhaps six families, were often out of order. The landlords, receiving very low rents and with slum clearance ahead, did almost no repairs. I heard constant complaints that 'he don't do nothing'.

Everywhere there was poverty. The lucky men who were employed earned only a pound or two a week. Those labouring for the Council got, I think, about three pounds a week; those in factories probably less. The factories closed for the 'August week' for stocktaking, but they did not pay their workers during the holiday. One old woman, taking out her provident money to see her through, said, 'Our bodies are in heaven but our minds are in hell.'

One winter afternoon I was in a kitchen when the father came in. He was a road worker, and in those days roads could not be mended in frosty weather. So he had been sent home. But he would not, he said, be paid for the idle period, and presumably, since he was in work, he would not get any unemployment benefit.

The old people had a pension of a few shillings a week, but you could not live on it, and few of them had ever earned enough to save anything. In winter occasionally people chopped up furniture because they had no coal for fires, or they kept warm by going to bed. They scamped their food in winter to buy fuel. 'It's better to be hungry than cold,' an old woman said to me.

They did, of course, misspend the money they had. The men and some of the women smoked cheap cigarettes and over-indulged in beer. They started smoking young. Alfie, aged eight, had always sucked a dummy. Now he went straight on to cigarettes. And there were all those pubs at corners – with nowhere else for the men to go. I was told of drunken fights on Saturday nights, though I never saw one, and people were hurt with bottles.

Once the Settlement asked me to take a questionnaire on incomes round the courts. But most of the wives said they did not know how much their husbands earned. ''E don't tell me. 'E gives me a bit and 'e keeps the rest for himself.' But some drunkards did not give their wives anything.

More money was wasted by pawning goods in an emergency, which meant extra money needed to get the goods out of pawn. If you were really desperate you bought something by hire purchase and then pawned it; but then you had two bills to pay.

Poverty separated families, for when they could the young ones moved out of Summer Lane, but then had to pay bus fares to visit their parents. And there was a general dread among the old people that they would not be buried decently. Often provident money was used for burial insurance when it should have been used for that expensive necessity – shoes.

Poverty makes lives very dull, especially if you cannot read. The children stayed at school to fourteen, but often could hardly read or write when they left. Education was not a subject we discussed in the Lane, and the only school exercise book I ever saw was from a local Roman Catholic school which seemed more concerned with teaching honour to the Virgin Mary than writing. The only school I heard praised, as will be mentioned later, was a special school for the mentally handicapped where the children stayed till sixteen and where the building was modern and bright. But that covered a wide area and had special funds.

It seemed that schools in the Summer Lane area had no hope of ever teaching much. The teachers knew what the homes were like and the impossibility of passing on any real education. Perhaps the teachers themselves, taking jobs in miserable areas, were not themselves of high quality.

Life in the courts must have been extremely uncomfortable, especially when there were large families. One family I knew had to serve meals in two sections because there were too many children to sit round the table together. There were still courts with only a communal tap in the centre. People were, of course, used to this, and one old lady refused to have water laid on in her kitchen when the landlord offered it. She did not want the workers in, and she said she had always got her water from the yard and she always would. For clothes-washing there was often a dank chilly 'brew-us' with a dilapidated sink in the court, but drying had to be done in lines across the kitchen.

Health generally was not as good as in the polite western suburbs. The air must have been polluted, though we did not talk of pollution in those days. I remember getting completely lost in a winter fog at the wide end of Summer Lane; standing in the road and not knowing which way to turn. Up the hill in the centre of the town the fog was not as thick. It was not only all those chimneys round the Lane. It was the lack of trees. On dry days there was blowing dust, and when rain came there were standing greasy puddles. Children and old people suffered from bronchitis, coughs and other chest complaints.

As I went round in the afternoons I did not see much of meals except for the slops of tea on the tables and the children running in and crying, 'Gi' us a piece, mom,' and being given a slice of white bread smeared with jam. Probably only white bread was sold in the food shops. It was cheaper than brown anyhow. The diet seemed to be unhealthy generally, with cheap bits of meat, milk out of tins and hardly any vegetables except potatoes and tinned peas. Tea was made strong and accompanied by spoonfuls of sugar. The children had plenty of sweets and tended to eat their food standing.

The large families had a bad effect on health in two ways. When babies came quickly there was not time for proper mothering, and meanwhile the half-houses soon became overcrowded. Women got bulky shapeless figures through too much child-bearing and lived in a state of constant dread of pregnancy. One mother of nine children told me she had swallowed pins as well as old wives' potions to bring on a miscarriage. 'But I ended,' she said, 'by upsetting my insides and had to go to hospital.'

Most babies seemed well and of average weight when they were born, and the mothers breast fed them as that was cheap. But the toddlers grew pale and undersized with running noses. Sick children were generally kept on hard old settees in the kitchen. ''E won't stay in bed,' the mothers would explain, and so the invalids were blown on by draughts from the door and probably passed on their illness if it was infectious. But they may have been better off downstairs than in a dark closed-up bedroom with bugs in the walls.

This was before the Health Service, but the working classes could get free treatment if they were 'on the panel'. They had to reach the doctor on foot, however, whether they were fit to walk or not, and they were rewarded with only bottles of medicine. Antibiotics had not arrived.

They could also get help from hospital casualty departments if they did not mind waiting. One mother with a large family who had taken a child to the Eye Hospital had to wait seven hours – of course without a meal.

Yet all the poverty and dirt and ill health did not obscure the feeling I gained of abundant life. The courts were full of birth and struggle and death. With early marriage families often ran to four generations. There were always children to be discussed. And one of the first things I noticed was the vigour of the language – when I understood it. The road was the 'horse-road'. The damp building for washing was a 'brew-us' from the day I suppose when beer was brewed. The dustbin was a 'miskin' and hands 'donnies'. 'Wave a donny' the adult carrying a baby would command when you parted from her. Grandmothers were 'nannies', as they still are in some quarters, and if something overwhelmed you you got 'a eyeful'. There often seemed a hint of poetry in the Lane conversation. A baby was 'cheeky Charlie', and the men who came round to empty the lavatories before there was water in the courts were 'night sile men'.

Part of the richness was because all these people were in contact with each other, sharing their family events. Certainly I often heard the remark, 'I keep meself to meself,' where there had been some tiff, but generally the women, who had little housework to do because their houses were so small and standards were low, would stand on their doorsteps chatting. Some people had bad reputations, and quarrels would blow up, but on the whole, in this open kind of life, the women, at any rate, were very kind to one another, minding children and helping with sickness.

One woman, however, complained that neighbours were not as kind as they used to be. In the nostalgia from which we all suffer she said that State pensions had had a bad effect. 'Before, you didn't have nothing, but people helped you more.'

People towards the end of the period were beginning to be moved out from the Lane to new Council housing. It was not unusual for the older ones to ask to come back, and sometimes by working exchanges with other families they could return to the old ground. On a Council estate, with its rows of houses instead of courts, they could not stand the loneliness.

But the tower blocks were a form of deprivation yet to come.

Savers

The filthiest kitchen that I ever came across, where one could hardly breathe, belonged to an old man, a knocker-up, whose job was to go round in the morning and with a long stick to bang on windows and get early workers out of bed.

He wanted to join the 'Provident' because other people were doing it and there was a little distinction in belonging; but he only occasionally put in a penny. He lived alone, and his kitchen reeked of dirt, and the table was so slopped with messes that there was nowhere to write. I could talk to and occasionally help most of my savers, but he seemed deaf and witless and I could do nothing with him. He died a few months after I began visiting him.

As I went round in the afternoon I generally saw the women, but there was one man I met who was a complete contrast to the knocker-up. He was known as 'the Belgian' – not because he was Belgian but because Belgian refugees had come to England in the First World War. He was really a Czech.

Through the war he had met and married an English girl. He was not at all the type one would have expected in Summer Lane. He spoke a thick foreign English but was always extremely polite. So was his wife when I saw her. Their kitchen was always clean and he seemed to have plenty of money. He was at home when I called because he worked at night. He saved half-a-crown or even five shillings a week, a fortune in those days. He showed up the evils of the Lane but possibly did not have much contact with the neighbours. Anybody from another country was an enigma to them.

Otherwise I saw mainly women. One of the wealthiest was Mrs G. who also saved half-a-crown a week. She was a tiny middle-aged woman with spectacles, and she had an alert intelligence. She kept a tiny shop fronting on the Lane and lived with her husband, also a small man, who had a job, in the half-house above. She sold cheap draperies – thin cotton garments, blouses, babies' clothes – and went every few weeks to a warehouse in Birmingham to stock up. This meant that she knew the centre of the town in a way most of the people of the Lane did not.

When you entered her shop an enormous bell clanged overhead. The first thing you noticed was a glass bowl on a worn wooden counter. Mrs G. kept goldfish, and lavished a mother's affection on them. She had no children and wanted to love something. The dark little shop could not have been a very healthy spot for fish, and they died – though it may have been through old age. She was nearly in tears when the last one went.

Mrs Gl., a rosy-cheeked old woman living in a side street, had another comfort – vegetation. Her face was like a withered apple, and her accent was Irish rather than Midland. She was among a number of Irish in the Lane, but she was clean and frugal as some of the others were not.

Like most old people she liked to talk of her past. She had gone out to service in Ireland, met an English soldier, married him and come to Birmingham. She had had an unspecified number of children, but they had gone. And the soldier had turned out to be a drunkard, and she was not sorry when he died. But she had had extra bad luck. She had married again, and this man was also a drunkard. Now she was alone except for her plants.

She grew anything she could lay hands on – potatoes, beans, annuals from penny seed packets. One knew her doorway at the end of the court by the green in an old box on the windowsill. Once she had a string stretched up to her bedroom window with a bean plant twining up it. Some of the Lane dwellers who had plants went out with a shovel to scrape up horse manure from the road. There were still enough horses about for this. Mrs Gl. probably went out too.

I had been told that Birmingham people had the reputation for being good gardeners, and in the eighteenth century a ring of gardens surrounded the town. Mrs Gl. had come to Birmingham only by chance, but she carried on the tradition.

Dot was at the other end of life – a pretty little girl with a round face and neat dark bobbed hair. She lived alone with her mother as she was the youngest of the family and the others had married and gone. She stood out by her neat appearance and nice manners. She was intelligent too. She belonged to a club at the Settlement, and the Settlement said she was one of the best members.

She was under fourteen and still at school when I first knew her, and was often in the kitchen when I called for her mother's savings. Then I saw less of her, and the Settlement said she was not appearing there either. 'She's boy mad,' one of the organisers said. 'When they're at that stage all their old interests go. It's an end of development. You can't do anything with them.'

I asked after Dot when I went in to get her mother's threepence. The mother hedged for a time and said she was quite well. Then one afternoon, when Dot must have been about sixteen, the story came out. 'She's had to go away. She's in trouble.'

With a wry face the mother told me that she had known for some time that Dot was 'expecting'. 'There wasn't no sign of – you know – on her clothes.' And Dot had become 'a bad girl. She told me lies.' In the end when her time was near she had had to own up, and her mother, who had turned against her, had sent her away to an elder sister.

As far as I remember in all the story there was no discussion of the young man. These things just happened when girls were 'naughty', and the men often disappeared. There was not any compulsion to marry. Anyhow Dot was too young. Presumably the baby would be taken into the family. The tragedy was for the bright girl who had become dead to all interests except boys. I never saw Dot again.

It was tiring tramping round the courts and standing to hear family problems, but at the end of the afternoon I had a rest. The acquaintance grew gradually, beginning when I was asked to call in and see Mrs S., whose daughter Polly was out working but was already in the Provident scheme. I found a neat clean kitchen with a good fire in the stove and a small old woman with bright eyes who was like a bird. Her name, Mrs Spink, suited her.

Presently she was offering me a cup of tea. Then bread and butter also awaited me. In the end each week I sat down for half an hour in the kitchen, refreshing myself and talking before I returned to the Settlement with my bag of coppers. Polly was a good saver, generally leaving me half-a-crown a week, but the welcome, with its cup of tea, came from the old lady.

Comfortably relaxed after the long tramp, I heard her life story. She had been an orphan, brought up in a convent which had left her with a great sense of cleanliness and decency, and a respect for education. But the nuns, she said, had been poor and she had never had enough food and been frequently ill, which had stunted her growth. She must have been not much more than four feet tall. But she had earned her living till middle age, and then Mr Spink had asked her to be his second wife.

'I wasn't in love with him,' she told me, 'but he had two daughters and wanted help.' Now he was dead, and one daughter was married and Mrs Spink lived with Polly.

Polly herself was a middle-aged neat woman working in a factory. I saw her now and then when she was on holiday, and she was very agreeable. Mrs Spink said that she was cross sometimes, and they kept their finances separate, but they needed one another and rubbed along fairly comfortably.

I did not talk to Mrs Spink only about her past. We discussed Roman Catholicism. She was still a Catholic but was critical of some of its practices. Up the hill from Summer Lane was Birmingham's Roman Catholic cathedral, St Chad's, well known for its design by the noted Victorian architect A. W. N. Pugin. Mrs Spink said that the wild young Irish men in the Lane went there for confession on Sunday morning and, having done their duty, fell to fighting on the steps outside.

Her problem was, as usual, money. She could not live on the few shillings a week provided by the State pension. She had saved what was then the immense sum of £400, but she was gradually using it up. She was now over seventy, but she was terrified that all her savings would be gone before she died. The 1930s did not have many sheltered homes for old people – except, of course, the historic almshouses.

Mrs Spink's problem was solved when she was a little over eighty. She died in hospital when she still had a few pounds left. And I had a gift from her that I should never have expected from Summer Lane – the complete works of Dickens in heavy illustrated Victorian volumes. She had them in her kitchen and said she wanted me to take them, and I picked them up, a few volumes at a time. I still have them.

Polly the daughter continued to write occasionally after I returned to London. She retired from work, and by that time there was an old people's home where she could live. She died there.

I had one more unusual picking from the Lane. I once passed a dirty little secondhand shop and saw a large framed print of Leonardo's 'Virgin with St Anne'. I had already bought, for some pounds, a reproduction of this cartoon for my office room, but I could not bear to see Leonardo in that dirty shop jumble. Who on earth in industrial Birmingham had been interested in this master work? I did not know, but, not considering the livestock I might import with it, I went in and bought it. It did not bring me any bugs and it cost ninepence.

Leisure

When I arrived in Birmingham the inhabitants stressed two attractions – the Burne-Jones windows in the cathedral and the fine country outside. But people who had come from other parts, particularly London, said it was an ugly, dirty place with standoffish people and no night life, and they hated it. I seemed to be the only stranger who did not want to return to London.

The beginning, however, was hard going, in spite of the efforts of Geo. W. I did not know a soul in the city, and I was working in the evening when most social events take place. I worked every other Sunday evening, and once a month, on a free weekend, went home to Surrey. Meanwhile I had hours and hours of time to fill up.

First I wrote to Birmingham University and asked if I could do a French degree. I received papers about courses, but, as I might have known, it was impossible for somebody working every evening. It might be easier today with the Open University. I was to find through the years that Birmingham University seemed to enter very little into the life that I knew. I went to one or two public lectures; met one or two of the staff; used a few articles from students. But the busy life of the city seemed mainly unaware of the activities in the building with its spacious tall tower at Edgbaston.

I dutifully looked at the Burne-Jones windows in the cathedral, in those days with its churchyard surrounded by heavy iron railings. They seemed to me forbidding, and I was glad when they were removed to be melted down when metal was needed in the war. The cathedral itself, with its eighteenth-century modesty, hardly seemed like a cathedral at all. St Martin's down the hill, then not cut off from the drab huddle of Digbeth, did at least give some feeling of the Middle Ages.

One wet Saturday afternoon I visited the Bull Ring because people said I should see it. Soaking pavements, flaring lights and parading crowds stretched away down the slope. At the kerb stood men with baskets shouting their wares. One was offering 'squeaking buns' to amuse or frighten people. I was attracted by some shining golden oranges and bought some. When I got home I found that they were completely dried up inside and had been painted.

I early visited the Art Gallery, also famous for its Pre-Raphaelites. In those days few special efforts were made to attract the public. The crowding international exhibitions, the workshops and school tours were to come after the war. I wandered in unhindered and found the large rooms with very few people going round. The tour was an easy one in those days with great Victorians, now restored to favour, offering their exquisite techniques and simple themes – Burne-Jones's Cophetua and the Beggarmaid, Millais's blind girl and the rainbow with plenty of lesser-known landscapes such as those by Wilson Steer. One did not have to make an effort in those days to accept contemporary European painting. I doubt if anybody much in Birmingham had heard of Picasso.

Before I had come to Birmingham one of the few things I had known about it was that it had a famous Repertory Theatre which was doing pioneering and highbrow work. But when I got there I found it was a small building in the drab quarter behind New Street Station, with people saying it could never make a profit because the auditorium was too small. Looking back, I am surprised now that I did not go there more frequently. I did see some performances, but I was always working in the evenings and much away at week-ends. It was the same with music at the Town Hall. It was not till the war had stirred us up and I was no longer working in the evening that I began to go to concerts.

I had arrived at the ugliest time of year, and Birmingham ugliness probably weighed on me. I remember how in spring I used to look out for Bournville's open spaces and crocuses when I was travelling by the Outer Circle bus, or what a lift of heart came when, after jerking by bus through dreary Sparkbrook, I began to see the first trees heralding Yardley. In my first Birmingham spring I began to long for the country, but there was nobody to walk with. So I walked alone once or twice – too early, for the country was still wintry.

Spring in the Midlands came about three weeks later than in the Thames Valley, and I was glad to get back to a fire.

But then Wag, the head printer, did invite me to the firm's sports ground, another benefit provided by our employer 'Charlie'. Wag was on the committee, and he said, "'Ere, we'll meet you.' The sports ground was at Yardley, the rural suburb where some of the printers lived. You went down a narrow passage, and a great green space spread before you with a pavilion at the end, and you could play tennis, bowls or other games or just sit about watching. Many people did sit about, for as yet there was no television to offer Saturday afternoon sports entertainment. Whole families would come along, and children would run about and wives would gossip.

The sports ground was an hour's journey, with two buses, from Edgbaston, but it filled up lonely Saturday afternoons. Sometimes I played tennis, but more often I sat with the wives, and, as a member of the editorial staff, was treated with deference. We nearly always talked of children and education, and my advice was solemnly asked. I hope I gave my opinions with sufficient dignity, for I felt a fraud all the time.

Later in the 'thirties Birmingham got a film society. These societies were springing up in cities to study the history and art of the cinema. The 'flicks' were still the main popular amusement of the nation, and every town had its garish cinemas. But these provided mainly low-brow American entertainment, while the high-brows wanted to study the cinema as an art form.

Down by the dark arches of Snow Hill Station we would go on a Sunday afternoon. In the cinema would be a scatter of university people, mainly young, teachers, members of one or two well-known liberal families, intelligentsia generally. It was not a social occasion as you could not meet people in the dark, but we saw a range of productions hailed as 'masterpieces' – the sinister German films made cheaply after the Great War, the famous Russian films with their crowd scenes but otherwise sluggish movement, the gentle René Clair comedies. As usual British talent seemed only minor, but there were Anthony Asquith, Robert O'Flaherty and John Grierson with his *Night Mail*, at the time pronounced to be brilliant, with words by Birmingham's own Wystan Auden. While international politics became ever more threatening, the film societies tranquilly enjoyed international cinema. The atmosphere was to be very different ten years later.

As time went on and I picked up acquaintances the burden of

loneliness lightened. I found to my surprise that there were already some women journalists in Birmingham – about half a dozen – and when I got to know the younger ones we would laugh together at the men who so much outnumbered us and compare notes on the way they treated us. But not all the women journalists were young. There was, for example, Godiva.

Tucked away in the Daily building were two rooms for the Weekly Post, which in an independent almost out-of-sight way belonged to the group. In one of the rooms sat Godiva, but anybody less like that legendary Coventry heroine, who rode through the street clothed only in her long hair, it would be difficult to imagine. No doubt the nom-de-plume had been adopted first because Godiva was an eminent Midland lady, and I think Miss L. had inherited it and now signed her weekly jottings with it. She was a fluttery white-haired lady with an over-genteel nervous voice. She told you at once that she was half French as a mark of distinction. How long she had been Godiva I did not know, but she was kind and took me out to lunch, and invited me to visit her at Glastonbury when she retired.

I must have been a trouble to my various hosts because of my odd sleeping hours. People did not understand that you cannot at will fall asleep four or five hours earlier than usual. 'You shall have an early night for once,' they would say kindly, and I would know that I was in for hours of insomnia and then have to get up when I was sodden with sleep.

But some of my younger hosts would be tempted to sit up with me over the fire to the early hours while we discussed life and its sorrows. At two o'clock, the fire would have fallen in and we would have talked ourselves to a standstill. Then my host would stagger up to bed and be tired for all the next day.

One such indulgent hostess was a teacher of Latin who lived five minutes from my last flat. Occasionally on Saturday nights we would sit in her flat relieving our souls of their burdens till all the house lights had gone out round us. Finally we had to stop, and I would hurry away, my steps ringing hollow in the silent streets. But it was a relief to talk of the emotional problems that afflict youth, and as I returned to my flat with a sense of freedom the stars would seem important, as they had seemed in childhood.

Moving

After I had lived at the Settlement for some months a woman journalist asked me if I would like to take over her flat as she was getting married. I went to visit her on a dark winter evening when I could not see much of the road but noticed, with deep relief, trees and hedges. The flat was on the first floor of a largish house in a side road from the straight Hagley Road in Edgbaston, and Gladys and her fiancé welcomed me in a warm room of low lights and cushions. It seemed luxurious after the bare Settlement, and they gave me supper and I felt the attraction of having your own rooms where nobody – so I thought – could interfere with you.

At the Settlement I was simply not getting enough sleep. Then a student laughingly told me that she could hear my footsteps coming up the Lane every night, and I realised that I was disturbing other people too. That decided me. I went to the wardens, who surprised me by saying that they had not expected me to stay long anyhow. But we were quite amicable, and I said I would continue with my 'Provident' round.

I had just inherited some furniture and had money to buy more. I should have to cater for myself, but I should be among trees again, and, the chief inducement, I should be – so I thought – able to sleep undisturbed. Almost the only advice Gladys gave me when she left was, 'Beware of Mrs J.' – the landlady who inhabited the ground floor of the house. 'She'll talk your head off.'

The road, seen in winter daylight, was rather decayed-looking, with straggly trees and overgrown privet hedges. The red brick houses appeared damp and secret. Many were probably let as flats. The only one I ever visited was Hope Lodge, where I went to write an article. It had a pious name as it was a home for unmarried mothers.

The flat, without Gladys's cushions, was a little damp and cold, and consisted of a large room and a small kitchen running the width of the house. In front it looked on to the road and, behind, to an unkempt bit of garden with a worn patch of grass. I had no idea who was in the house. I had seen only the affable fat landlady who guarded the front door and handed over a large key.

So I began to travel home by office coach again, leaving it at 1.00 a.m. and penetrating the overgrown empty side road. Nobody was about, but once I thought I heard a child crying in a garden. Here was a problem. What should one do? I opened a gate and went into a black front garden, and then suddenly a cat dashed out, and I realised that I had been deceived by its love song. But it was the sort of street that might have had secrets.

I soon found that a flat in a converted house is not noiseless. In the Birmingham of the 'thirties large family houses were being partitioned into flats but without much attempt at sound-proofing. The heyday of the purpose-built block of flats with insulated ceilings and walls did not come till after the war, and during the 'thirties flats were mainly carved from large buildings no longer wanted because families were smaller. The noise problem, as far as I remember, was hardly discussed, yet it must have caused much exasperation.

There were bumps overhead in my new flat, and clattering steps passed my door and went down the common staircase. I was told presently that a teacher and someone else lived in the unknown top of the house, but I hardly saw them. But Mrs J., the landlady, was at the bottom all day as flat-dwellers came and went. She had a room, cluttered with furniture, by the door, and when she heard people going by she peeped out and had a conversation. She had many conversations with me as I was there when other people were out.

With greasy black greying hair and a drooping fat figure, she soon told me of her troubles. She had been deserted by her husband, and now she did not know how she was going to pay her bills. Her conversations were long laments. She had a daughter of seventeen, quiet and pale, who went to work in a shop. 'A good kid,' said Mrs B. who was on my floor across the landing, but we saw little of her.

After many conversations I began to tiptoe past our landlady's door. Then she began to come up and tap on mine, making small pretexts such as: Could she borrow some scissors? I began to feel hunted. Mrs B. across the landing declared that Mrs J. was a nuisance; so I locked my door and did not answer when she tapped.

I knew that I was being unreasonable. If she had been one of my Summer Lane people I should have listened with sympathy and felt that I was doing good. But I was less kind when my own comfort was threatened.

Meanwhile the noise problem had appeared again. Mr B. across the landing made a rumpus in the morning. He banged his flat door, ran down the stairs and banged the front door – always in the same way. Later I would get up and go to the chilly bathroom with the old geyser for a bath, and there in the bath would be a sprinkling of grit and soil.

Once or twice I met Mrs B. coming out of the bathroom with her potatoes, and she told me that she washed them in the bath. That explained the soil; and she too was anxious to talk. She was young, dark and heavily made up, and not, she told me, used to keeping house. Before her marriage she had been in a London office, and she and Mr B. were both Londoners and hated Birmingham. Mr B.'s firm had sent him there, and now she had no friends and little to do. 'I don't know a soul here,' she said, 'and don't want to. We're both longing to get back.'

She must have grown very confiding, for she told me that she did not want 'any little fair-haired babies'. (Mr B. was fair.) But she had no babies at all at the moment; only a small Peke which she addressed in toddler language and carried about under her arm. She took it out in the afternoon, shopped, kept two rooms dusted and prepared an evening meal. In the morning she trailed round in a picturesque pink dressing-gown. That was her life in Birmingham.

Downstairs there was a family with other troubles. They lived at the back and in the basement at reduced rates because Mr S., who had lost his work in the slump, did odd jobs about the house. They had pretty little identical twins, exactly alike, aged two; but I got to know them only slowly as Mrs S., a pale anxious young woman, was afraid that they would annoy us and was always chasing them into her back room and closing the door. I glanced in once, and it was almost empty except for a clothes horse.

Mrs S. cooked in the basement, which may have been dark. She did not look as if she got enough to eat. Mr S. was also small and worried but inclined to be boastful as one who is at a disadvantage. He had had an office job and did not seem able to find another.

Presently Mrs S. began to talk about the children, who, for me, cheered up the house. They were already beginning to play tricks, she said, one pretending to be the other. She was the only one who could tell them apart. Their father could not.

So the lives in the house were being poisoned by boredom and poverty. Possibly it might not be so bad today. The bored Mrs B. could have got a job and there would have been more money and opportunities for the S.s.

I went and came for some months. Then Mrs B. across the landing began to talk of the troubles of the house, and it seemed almost the Mayfield situation over again. Our landlady, Mrs B. said, had not the money to maintain the house. 'She was a fool to take it. She can't possibly keep it going on her income. But' – and there was a note of triumph in her voice – 'it doesn't matter to us as we're going back to London.'

Mrs J. now seemed permanently near tears, and this was embarrassing and I avoided her more than ever. The people on the top floor disappeared, and there was a heavenly silence. But Mrs B. said that, without the rent from the top, a crisis had come in Mrs J.'s affairs.

One morning there was a knock on my door, and little Mr S., the unemployed man from below, appeared. He said he had a proposition to make. Mrs J. was being forced to sell the house; so why didn't we all club together and buy it? We could get more people for the top, and we should have our own rooms and have the rents from the other flats. He would manage everything and act as janitor.

I was flattered that he should appeal to me, but Mrs B. across the landing was contemptuous. 'The S.s haven't a penny to bless themselves with. How is he going to pay for the repairs? And who wants to live in this old dump anyhow? He's only trying to make a job for himself.'

Autumn was coming again – Birmingham's sharp wet autumn when one wanted a secure home. I must have talked about my housing problem in the office, for somebody showed me an advertisement in our evening paper offering an Edgbaston flat about a mile further out. The owner was looking for an unmarried educated lady as he had other ladies in the house. This sounded a bit strange, but I made enquiries and found that the advertiser was, as I might have expected, old. But with his drooping moustache, Birmingham accent and humble manner, he was obliging too. I decided that I would move once again.

I did not dare to speak to Mrs J., the landlady. I sent her a note, and she must have given up hope, for she did not answer or try to see me. The B.s had also given notice and were going into a hotel till they got back to London. I did not know what the S. family was doing, but I hoped something would turn up for them.

Then we heard that Mrs J. was selling up and going into rooms. We felt sorry for the quiet little daughter. A removal van came for my furniture, and I had to tap on Mrs J.'s door to give back the key. She was quite subdued; took it and said almost nothing. Her eyes were dim with crying.

I used to pass the side road when I went into Birmingham by bus, and for a time I had a faint sense of guilt. I had not been very kind to Mrs J. Then in a year or two I forgot her.

Pimmy Etc.

I did not meet many notable people in Birmingham – only politicians on elections nights, members of the Cadbury family at meetings and one or two minor writers. I suppose the Auden family were to become the most outstanding of my new acquaintances, but at the time I had no inkling of the high claims that were to be made for Wystan.

The meeting came through Dr G. A. Auden, who was medical inspector of schools for Birmingham. One afternoon I visited some school to write an article about it, and he was there. He must have been a stimulating conversationalist, as well as genial, for we began to talk about Birmingham history, and talked for most of the afternoon.

Soon afterwards I had an invitation to tea from Mrs Auden. She was elderly and benevolent and told me about her worries over one of her three sons, Wystan. He was an unbeliever, hostile to all that she cherished. Yet she proudly showed me a book of his verse with an inscription to her.

I went to see her several times and met Wystan. He was uncouth and silent, obviously ill at ease, and he did not bother about his mother's guest. I thought him rude, and I remember walking along a road with him on my way back to Birmingham and wondering how to carry on a conversation. I had some idea that he was becoming a cult figure at Birmingham University, but I had also heard that he had scorned Romantic poetry when he was at Oxford and mocked at 'Sheats' and 'Kelley'. In my juvenile judgment this would have been impossible in a true poet. I knew nothing of his homosexuality, and I should have been amazed if I had been told that he would become one of the salient figures of the 'thirties. But I did like his father.

It is always easier, of course, to converse with humbler characters, and I had plenty of talk at the office. There, most obliging of all, was Pimmy, the small printer who made up my page. But the relationship did not end at the office. It was not long before he was inviting me to visit his wife at Yardley. 'Lil says will you come over one Saturday? Just when you're free, like.'

I do not know how many times I went out to that small house. I continued to go after I had left the Daily in the war and once after I had returned to Surrey. When I first knew Yardley it still had a country atmosphere, though small red houses, including Pimmy's own, were already eating up the fields. The firm's playing field was there, and other sports fields preserved some open spaces.

Pimmy would always be waiting for me at the bus terminus under a grove of magnificent trees. A path full of puddles led along the side of a large expanse of green playing field. Pimmy's house was in a thin line of houses facing the green, with other printers living near and one village shop. Outside his house an oak had been left, adding to the country atmosphere. He had a neat front garden screened by the tree.

The fresh-faced Lil would be waiting, but the little boy would generally be at Cubs. Lil's health was not good. Her 'insides', she told me, had been wrecked when she had Norman. They had let him get too big, and he was twelve pounds born. Since then she had had a series of operations. They did not manage obstetrics so well in the 1920s.

Lil generally had a bright fire, for Birmingham was chilly most of the year and a mark of hospitality was to put on plenty of coal. But before tea Pimmy would take me down his back garden. It was very long, reclaimed from a field, with only lines of wire to separate it from neighbours' grounds. But they all seemed to get on well together. Pimmy kept his strip in excellent order, with roses near the house, then vegetables, then young fruit trees.

Though he was a very good gardener, his knowledge of horticulture was hazy in a way that would be unlikely today with all the gardening articles and television programmes. I remember his telling me during the war, when so many people began to grow tomatoes as a new venture, that if you left a tomato plant long enough in the ground it would turn into a potato. He celebrated the coronation of George VI in 1937 by planting an oak sapling half way down the garden. If it is still there it must be causing a large obstruction.

Tea was the lavish visitors' meal of the period – thin slices of white bread with thick yellow butter, lettuce and tomatoes, jam, homemade cakes including a sponge with thick jam, fruit salad and tinned cream, all with strong tea – a mixture which gave me indigestion. During the meal and afterwards we sat in the warm little back room and talked of the office and other printers' families.

Once or twice in the summer Lil and Pimmy took me for a walk.

At the beginning there were meadows at the end of their road, but presently they wanted to show me the large building programme that had begun. The fields were still yellow with birdfoot trefoil, but foundations of dozens of small boxlike houses were visible; rough roads were appearing and trees were being cut down. My Yardley has now gone.

It was generally Saturday when I went to tea with Pimmy. During tea a paper-boy would thrust the local sports sheet through the door, and Pimmy would glance at it and then put it aside for the evening's reading. Between six and seven he would go into the garden to cut me a cabbage or pick me apples, and then he would conduct me back to the bus-stop and then repair to the local pub for a beer.

He did not live to be very old. Night work took its toll with most of the printers in the way of indigestion and boils, and it may have affected him. His day and night were cut into small slices. He would get home at something after 1.00 a.m. or about five if he was on the late shift. He would have a smoke, go to bed for a few hours, get up in mid-morning to do his garden and then have an afternoon rest. He seldom had a normal spell of sleep. But perhaps his work, for which he had served a seven-year apprenticeship, was more interesting than most. He earned about four pounds a week, by 'Charlie's' beneficence more than the trade union rate.

Lil did not live very long either, but the small son did well.

Flat at a Corner

Mr E., the old man who wanted to devote his house to educated ladies, had some small business which kept him in comfortable circumstances. He had bought the building in an outer part of Edgbaston where the dwellings were not as affluent and imposing as those near Five Ways. It was a wilderness of bright red slate-roofed respectable houses with small front gardens, and it bordered on to the industrial wasteland of Smethwick (Smerick in local speech). Beyond, colonies of small new houses extended westward.

Mr E., who took me round his house, explained that he had bought it for his wife, but she had not liked it. So he had bought another for her and decided to let this out as flats. There were already two ladies, one working in a bank, downstairs. I could have the first floor, and there was a large top room up a winding stair – a fire trap if there ever was one but nobody thought much of that in those days before the war.

Mr E. was very anxious to make us comfortable. He did not trust electricity; so, though he had it installed, he left the old gaslight fittings in case the electric light should fail us. He offered me two bedrooms, a huge sitting-room, a large kitchen (a converted bedroom) and a bathroom, not as a closed-in unit but spread out along an open passage. He was full of good will, but presumably had not had advice on converting the house. He had put a sink and two open wooden shelves in the bedroom that was to be my kitchen. The large sitting-room and bedroom had gas fires, but the fire in the sitting-room was far too small to heat the room in cold weather. I was later to huddle by the fire in the winter and, when visitors came, put the chairs in a semicircle at the warm end, while I grew hyacinths in pots at the two windows facing different ways. We were not used to the comfort of central heating in those days.

But old Mr E. had done nothing to solve our noise problem. Perhaps nothing could have been done. The ceilings were like drums. I was in the middle, and loud wireless music would rise from the ladies below, while, above, thumps and bangs went on till late into the night. That top room drew several solitary women. One had a cat called Corrie after George VI's coronation. It was not let out, and its needs were not met adequately. I would smell a strong cat whiff and look up and see a pale yellow patch spreading on my ceiling. Presently the ceiling had a pattern of pale yellow patches.

No doubt my night hours caused disturbance to the others. We were all too unprotected from one another. Once, when some friends of mine stayed late on a Saturday, the lady below knocked and said she could not sleep. There was trouble when splashes from my bathroom seeped through the ceiling below. It must have been a very flimsy house. At one time the strange woman above used to kick my door as she went by in the morning because I had asked if she could be a little quieter.

But the disagreements were spread over years, and when air raids came we linked up and grew friendly. The deficiencies of the house mattered less because we were out at work at different times. And my rooms had one advantage. A building had been pulled down across the road leaving a small wilderness, and I could look out on some trees and now and then a white butterfly.

However, it was a life almost completely detached from the life of the road – a suburb that had no centre. For a long time I knew nothing of the inhabitants of the buildings round. Then somebody asked me to visit a housebound old lady in the side road, and there was my teacher friend a few minutes' walk away. And when I got a car I garaged it in the yard of a nearby factory. Otherwise nobody in the street knew me and I knew nobody. It was a situation which must have been repeated hundreds of times in cities before the war. The war loosened us, but presumably people living on their own in boxlike dwellings are still plagued by loneliness.

I had melancholy moments when I was in on winter Saturday afternoons, when twilight came before the lamps suddenly flickered out mauve and green. And on summer nights I longed for fields or gardens far from the endless streets of red houses. One night I went out to look for green spaces and walked a long way, but the best I could find was a small park shut behind railings. A few trees stretched over the street and they held some tranquillity, but I was afraid of being seen and went home again.

But I had moved house enough and I was busy. So, even while I declared that I would never live in a flat off the ground again, I stayed on.

My rent remained the same through the years – twenty-six shillings a week.

Charlie's Treats

'Charlie' provided us with two entertainments a year – a summer garden party and a winter dance. For each we received large card invitations, and he must have spent hundreds of pounds on us each year. We hardly ever saw him otherwise, but at his parties one could view him – a plump middle-aged man, closely consorting with his male editorial staff and apparently shy of the work people he treated so lavishly.

There was some excitement in the office before the Saturday entertainments. The printers looked forward to a day of pleasure, but leader writers and sub-editors were rather embarrassed at it. It was a very paternal entertainment such as a squire might give to the workers on his estate, and there was still a gap between the office staff and the 'hands'.

The garden party was held on Charlie's estate at Berkswell, and everything possible was provided for our comfort. Coaches waited in the centre of Birmingham for those who had no cars. We raced along the main road towards Coventry and then turned off into country lanes. The July weather generally seemed to be bad, with rain and wind, but a huge marquee had been set up with rows of white-clothed tables, and in there it was warm with the sweet smell of trodden grass. We were each given a carnation to pin to our lapels. Sir Charles sat at a cross table with his chief henchmen, and the rest of us fitted in as we liked.

Deferential waiters stooped over us with food. We had chicken (a luxury in those days) and salad, and then an ice-cream pudding followed by coffee. Afterwards the marquee filled with a haze of smoke from all the cigarettes. Then Sir Charles made a short speech inviting us to wander as we pleased. If the weather allowed there was a cricket match between the editorial staff and the rest, and we could watch that or visit the rose garden or the library. A band played, and, if on a rainy afternoon the time passed a little slowly, a tea of strawberries and cream lay ahead.

After tea came balloon time. We assembled outside, and kindly men provided each of us with a balloon which had a label on which we wrote our name. There was apparatus for blowing the balloons up and sealing them, and then we let them go, and they went up, up to the heavens. I remember a moment when, after a wet afternoon, the clouds suddenly parted and the sun came out and the great flock of coloured balloons went heading off with the wind. There was a sparkle over everything.

The person whose balloon was found farthest away would have a prize, but nobody I knew got one. The balloons were a signal for families with young children to wander to an early coach, though the band was still playing and fireworks were promised. But most of the editorial staff left early too.

It was a munificent entertainment reminding me of Tennyson, and yet once I had a shock. A few of us had left the crowd and walked across a field, and there we met a gamekeeper who began to talk.

He told us that Sir Charles would soon be entertaining a shooting party. The keeper, in spite of his job, did not 'hold' with this. He said that the whole system was shockingly expensive, and each bird you shot cost a fortune. Also it was cruel. 'You bring the young birds up, give them every comfort, make pets of them – and then kill them for sport.'

The friendliest birds, he said, were always shot first. One year he had reared a particularly affectionate partridge 'and made a real pet of it. It always came when it heard me. I loved that bird. At the shoot it came flying straight out to greet the party, and it was the first to drop.'

Sobered by this tale we returned, and the world did not seem quite as idyllic.

The winter dance, held soon after Christmas in Birmingham's Grand Hotel, was also paternal and divided the guests according to status. The editorial group, with wives and men from the London office, were given a dinner first. The printers and lower orders had just the dance. Yet it was the lower orders who were enthusiastic while the top people were a little embarrassed.

We assembled in evening dress after powdering and hair arrangement in the warm cloakroom. Our names were by our places at table, and we were all very affable. The wives were freer than the men, and tended to tell stories about their husbands. 'Eric's a perfect fool in the house,' said the wife of the distinguished music critic. 'He can't even mend a fuse.' Meanwhile the men in their evening suits were rather silent or made little remarks *sotto voce* to one another.

The meal was lavish and lasted nearly an hour, and then we rose to join the dancers in the hotel's large ballroom. The dance was well under way with the band thumping, faces red and boys and girls gliding and curveting. My first impression was always that it was a dance of strangers, for staffs from other papers of the group had come in, and girls had brought fiancés and other employees their families. But presently I caught sight of a face or two I knew, and we greeted one another warmly like friends in a strange multitude. Then there was the old business of grins, handshakes, 'Let me introduce my wife', and then the talk about children and schools.

The editorial staff danced little but stood at the sides, smiling affably and conversing with one another. Now and then somebody, often a stranger, invited me to dance, but I was taller than some of those small men and my dancing was not expert. Drink flowed freely, and presently one noticed a stagger or two, crimson faces and raucous laughter. It remained an event mostly for the humbler side of the firm, and the editorial group, with members of the London staff who might be staying the night with them, began to catch one another's eye and move to the door.

I would be lucky if someone offered me a lift in his car. Down the wide steps over soft carpets we would go to the raw gleaming street, and the cold would hit us and possibly a little relief that the entertainment was over.

How free and uninhibited we felt the next evening when we were back at work at the office.

Garden Openings

'I wonder,' Geo. W. said at the beginning of my first April in Birmingham, 'if you could do something with this?' He showed me a thin booklet. 'I'd like to help them if I could.'

The booklet had been issued by the Queen's Institute of District Nursing which, before the coming of the National Health Service, had to find money for itself. It was persuading local landowners to open their gardens in aid of district nursing, with a charge of a shilling or sometimes sixpence. The booklet gave the programme for 1930, and it showed that one or two gardens near Birmingham were to be opened.

At that time the great estates round Britain were unknown to the public except perhaps for local events. They were shut away behind gates and avenues, and the public was not aware of them. There was no cult of garden visiting and, of course, comparatively few cars to reach the gardens.

When Geo. W. brought me the booklet I had heard only vaguely of the Queen's Institute. 'Get in touch with Mr Cole,' Geo. W. said. Mr Cole, another George, was the Daily's chief photographer, and he had previously gone with me out to the British Industries Fair at Castle Bromwich. 'Choose a garden fairly near,' Geo. W. said, 'and write to the owners and ask if you can look round before the opening. You can do a note, and Mr Cole can take a photograph. I'll write and tell the Queen's Institute that we'll help.'

So began our garden trips that continued each summer till the war. They grew longer as time went on, as we used up all the gardens near Birmingham. We went right out to the Welsh border and into Oxfordshire. But it was a useful idea. The Queen's Institute and the garden-owners were pleased, and we could fall back on garden photographs for the women's page on blank days.

I found how rich the Midlands were in great houses – mediaeval foundations, priests' hiding holes, Adam ceilings, Capability Brown gardens. There were more of them then, of course, before the post-war demolitions, and more in private hands. On that first April we began with a Worcestershire property opening for its daffodils. Of course I loved flowers, and I became lyrical about them and then, as the season moved on, about warm kitchen gardens scented with apple blossom, massed delphiniums and lilies in borders, rustic bridges over waterlily ponds and heavy clusters of grapes in glass houses.

But one cannot go on with flower delight for ever. Presently I curbed poetic flights and began to delve into history – battles, connections with famous men. My descriptions grew to hundreds of words, enough to discourage any reader in a hurry. But George took fine pictures, and our publicity did increase visitors to the gardens.

Each spring I had the Queen's Institute booklet and fixed our visits for some day before each garden opened. We went out fortnightly till August when George had his holidays. As mine followed in September, that was the end of our season. On excursion days I got up earlier than usual and went straight in to town. At the back entrance of the office George would be in his car studying maps.

There was an extra amusement in going out with a press photographer, for he looked, as we went along, for subjects for pictures. Local views were wanted, as they made the Birmingham papers different from the nationals. As we bowled into the country I kept my eyes open for subjects. Unfortunately the views I suggested did not always appeal to George. 'Oh look! Do take that!' I would cry as a horse poked its nose over a fence under a hawthorn tree.

'Nothing in it,' George would say drily, driving on.

'It's a spring picture.'

'My dear girl, there are lots of horses and trees about.'

But he would stop in the Vale of Evesham to take pictures of plum blossom, often with daffodils growing round the trees. I had heard early about the Evesham blossom and how Birmingham people made excursions to see it. It seemed, in those days, of exquisite beauty after Birmingham. But George, true to his trade, always tried to introduce a girl or animals into the picture to give it 'life'.

As we drove along we exchanged news of the office. George, working for three papers of the group, saw a wider slice of it than I did. Then, if conversation flagged, I asked him about the Great War. Like other men in the office he had been in the army and, like them, he was pleased to talk of it now that war seemed gone for ever. With all its fearfulness, which he described with complacency, it had brought a widening of experience. I expressed horror at his stories, and he rather liked that.

Summer rushed by as we made the excursions. On the first outing many trees would still be bare; on the third most would be in heavy summer leaf. Almost before we had fully realised that winter was over, hay would be made in the fields that were so much smaller than today's, and wild roses would be twining in the hedges that were everywhere. Almost immediately the corn, still in those days dotted with red poppies, would be ripe, and then it would be, 'Have nice holidays. See you next year.'

Our reception at the great houses varied. Once we were sent round to the servants' entrance, but generally we were admitted at once to those halls smelling of age and floor polish, with walls decorated with animal heads. Great jars of flowers stood on the floor, and copies of the *Bystander* and *Country Life* were spread out on low tables. Several times we were given tea in elegant drawing rooms, with heavy silver teaspoons balanced on small porcelain saucers and with strong tea and rich fruit cake.

George hated to be told what to photograph; so he went off on his own if he could. It was generally the lady of the house or the head gardener who took me round. The master usually attended to larger aspects of the estate. I remember, however, one landowner walking me round and pointing to two ears pricking above the greenery. 'My pet fox,' he said. 'Rescued him young. He always follows me about.'

I suppose that he hunted, but I did not ask. Hunting was an absolutely established amusement, and you would have been thought a crank if you had questioned it. Nearly all the houses we visited had large and small dogs running round, almost as if we were still in the eighteenth century.

The owners frequently complained about the difficulty of getting labour and of the rise in wages, but there always seemed to be plenty of retainers about. Also, there often seemed some tension between the lady of the house and the head gardener, and they would make mild complaints of one another. Each felt that the gardens were his personal property, and they had different ideas on what should be planted. The lady hinted that 'he' behaved as if the place belonged to him. The gardener, who often had a rural voice that would have delighted Shakespeare, said that 'she' was awkward and sometimes didn't know what she was talking about. It was a closed community without much amusement, with towns far away – and most of the 'gentry' hated Birmingham anyhow – so that it was easy for tiffs to break out.

One thing surprised me. Families that had owned estates for centuries knew little about their history. Indeed they knew little history at all. Living on country estates, apparently, did not improve brains. The men were particularly ignorant. The ladies who had married into the family often knew more than their husbands. The best informed owners were rich business people who had recently bought properties.

Once or twice we were sent round to the local clergyman as the source of local history. I remember a long wait outside an old brick house near the church and a shabby old man emerging suspiciously at last. He warmed when I asked about history and he offered a pamphlet he had written. 'The people round here are very ignorant,' he said. 'They don't care at all for the past.' But his pamphlet on the church was dry as dust, monotonously plodding through dates.

Sometimes we were sent to look at a family tomb and peeped into small decaying churches. Grass and nettles were high in the churchyards. We might push open a heavy door and see a crumbling painting on the walls, or a man scything the grass might tell us that the tower was unsafe. Church decay was accepted in the 'thirties. The neo-Gothic architects of Victorian times had swept away much mediaeval rot in larger churches and substituted works of their own. Now they were out of favour and the 'thirties had other problems than church decay. It was the bombing to come that would make the public interested in antique small buildings. The Churches' Conservation Trust, formerly the Redundant Churches' Fund, did not come till after the war.

George would always finish first, having taken about half a dozen photographs. He would retire and sit patiently smoking in the car. After I joined him and the formal farewell was over would come the best moment of the day. We would drive away to the nearest town, find a café and have tea at the office's expense. After an early rising, a journey, say, of fifty miles and more than an hour of walking round an estate on a gusty day, I would find the hot tea, bright magenta or chocolate cakes and warm shelter blissful; and behind us would be the job done.

Then back we would race to Birmingham so that I could be punctual for the evening's work. George, who after all had done all the driving, would be free to go home.

Ghosts

The first Midland ghosts I heard about were in Moseley, Birmingham.

Mr L.P.H., the assistant editor who put sarcastic notices in green ink on my desk, would wander in early on some evenings for a brief discourse. He always carried a pipe and panted slightly, I suppose through over-smoking, and he would make small dry remarks and was apparently amused at my youth. But one day he launched into a story – I did not know why – except that the incident may have just happened.

He said that there was a respectable old man in Moseley, well known as a local character. For many years he had been seen about the streets, and one morning Mr L.P.H., walking by a long wall, met him with his wife. 'We said good morning,' Mr L.P.H. told me, 'and I walked on. Then suddenly I remembered, "That man's dead." And his wife? "But she's dead too." I turned, and there was the long wall behind, and not a sign of anybody. No. There were no turnings.'

In 1931 the fourth edition of *An Adventure* was published. It was an account of how two Oxford women, Charlotte Anne Elizabeth Moberly and Eleanor Frances Jourdain, visited Versailles and slipped back to the time of Marie Antoinette. There had been much discussion at the time as to whether the experiences were genuine or not, and we passed the book about and also discussed it. An Oxford friend told me that Miss Jourdain, who was later principal of St Hugh's College, Oxford, had other experiences of shifts in time and once was caught in an eighteenth-century crowd at Oxford going to see a hanging.

So even in the internationally troubled 'thirties we were discussing ghosts and slips in consciousness. I did not myself, however, meet Midland ghosts till one summer of garden visiting. Those old historic houses should have been able to serve up other-world experiences, but I was always with people and busy getting information. However one brooding July afternoon we drove out – not very far – to a house that went back to the Middle Ages, which later had been owned by Roman Catholic gentry. It was hidden away in the woods, and it was said that in the Civil Wars Cromwell marched to attack it but never found it. The old caretaker told me that there were still wild lilies of the valley in the woods, but begged me not to mention them for fear of Birmingham despoilers.

In those days massive elms studded the countryside, and here they flanked the moat of the ancient brick house. There was not much garden to see, but the house, too, was to be open. George said at once that a view over the moat was the obvious one, and he would not bother to go inside. The family was away, and only an old caretaker was in charge. But he offered to take me round.

Afterwards I could not quite remember what happened. The house was dim and silent with a sweetish scent of age and decay. The caretaker guided me upstairs, and we went through a series of rooms that confused me. They led from one to another and had four-poster beds. The place seemed breathless, and I began to feel curiously light-headed. In one room I thought I saw a white cat on a bed, but it was only a bit of tissue paper.

The caretaker was talking of ghosts. He said that some member of the family had imprisoned his wife in one of the rooms and then murdered her. She was still seen coming out of the room. He showed me the door and then led me into a pale upstairs hall running the width of the house with small lattice windows at each end. It was empty but warm with a low ceiling, light wooden floor and a curious brightness.

I went to one set of windows and looked out. There were the elms with their heavy foliage, dead still as if cut in stone. Behind me in the room something seemed to be going on. The air was thick, but it was not at all frightening – rather exciting and happy.

I said to the caretaker, 'Is this room haunted?'

'Are you psychic?' he asked.

It was not a word one used much in those days, and it seemed to have nothing to do with that curious thick radiance. Yet in a way I was flattered.

'No, I don't think so,' I said. I did not ask him if he felt this curious lightness too.

Then he told me there were other ghosts in the house beside the murdered lady. We were standing in the mediaeval banqueting hall, and it was certainly haunted. Visitors often said they could not sleep because of the voices and laughter.

'What? Recently?' I asked.

'Oh yes, all the time.'

As is usual with these experiences one is unwilling to go away and at the same time glad to escape to the commonplace world. The room was quite empty and there was nothing more to be seen; so the caretaker took me downstairs and we emerged on the hot still afternoon. George was sitting in the car smoking and waiting for me. Everything was as usual, and yet I felt I had stumbled on some great secret. But I said nothing.

The sight of Birmingham buses and shops was extraordinarily unpleasant – signs of a prison world. All that evening the exhilaration continued, and the next day I felt as if something important had happened. And then gradually I forgot the feeling.

All imagination? No. For a fortnight later I had a similar experience. This time we went almost to the Welsh border. As usual George wandered off on his own, and the lady of the house said she would take me round, as some of the rooms would be open.

It was, as far as I remember, an eighteenth-century house with lofty dim rooms. Vaguely as we stood in one of the bedrooms I felt the stirring of the previous excitement, a feeling of there being more there than we could see, and in me a vague light-headedness.

Again I asked, 'Is this room haunted?'

The effect was surprising. The lady stopped short. 'Please don't say anything,' she whispered.

Then in a low voice she told me that guests who slept in the large bed often saw a man pass through the room. There was a tragic story to explain his presence, but she concealed it. Above all, the servants must not know. 'They would leave us if they found out,' she said, 'and it's so difficult to get maids in this part of the country.'

Afterwards she begged me, 'You won't write anything about it, will you?' Of course I did not, but I knew again that sometimes one can sense something beyond the workaday world.

Whether visitors to these houses felt anything similar I, of course, never heard. Probably not. There would be crowds of them and they would be talking and making a great stir.

I never went back to either house. If I went now I should probably feel nothing at all. I have indeed half forgotten what I felt. All I have is the knowledge that these moments exist.

Visits

Gradually the unknown country round Birmingham began to open up. Sometimes I was sent out to 'cover', as newspapers say, local specialities. Sometimes I stayed with friends whom I had made through the paper.

Redditch was a very small town known for the needle trade. I went out to the factory and watched all the processes of turning a short length of metal into a needle with a point and an eye. Abbots Bromley was a Staffordshire village noted for its ancient horn dance through the street. I went out with one of the photographers to watch the procession with the great reindeer horns, which were generally kept in the church.

One aristocratic visit took nearly all day. People travelling along the Alcester Road could not help noticing the long front of Coughton Court with its avenue and central gatehouse. It now belongs to the National Trust, but in the 'thirties the Throckmorton family, who had been there since 1409, was still in possession.

I had been told stories about the house and how it had remained a Roman Catholic stronghold all through the years of persecution. Perhaps it was from Lady Throckmorton herself that I had the story of how Catholics concerned with the Gunpowder Plot sat at night in an upper room awaiting the sound of a rider from London who would tell them if the plot of blowing up Parliament had succeeded. They heard the galloping horse in the darkness, but the rider burst in and brought news of disaster. The plot was discovered, the conspirators · taken. The Catholic group at Coughton had to disappear into hiding.

I went out to Coughton for some kind of news story and met Lady Throckmorton, who insisted I should stay for lunch. I saw a way of life which was quite detached from ordinary plebeian existence. We are more used to these grand historic families now that their houses are regularly open, and I myself had other glimpses of it when we visited gardens, but it was new to me then. It was summer and as far as I remember there were silver bowls of roses about and much silver on a long table. Possibly a dozen people were there for lunch – friends and house guests – but the chief thing I remember was jugs of some beverage with blue flowers, borage, I think. The talk was of local matters – people of the neighbourhood enlightening me about the affairs of Warwickshire which might have ben a hundred miles from Birmingham.

After lunch I was instructed in other history. Lady Throckmorton took me round the house. On small tables were silver-framed portraits of men in fine uniforms and women in elegant Victorian dresses. The Throckmortons, as Catholics, were allied with Catholic nobility throughout Europe, and family history was part of national events. I should have followed it better if I had not been shy and in awe of this great family. As it was I departed with a glimpse of a world that I had hardly imagined before.

People who had sent me articles sometimes called at the Daily office. They were often not at all the types I had imagined. Among those who had sent me articles written in a large firm hand about Derbyshire history was Mrs M., tall, red-cheeked and calling herself a farmer's daughter. She explained that she had had no education but longed for learning, and would I, as a Cambridge graduate, come for a weekend? Later she confided that she had wanted her daughter to learn good English; so she had hung pages from Thomas Carlyle – of all people – up in the lavatory.

So one Saturday morning I took a train in a direction which seemed unnatural for Birmingham – north and east. Mrs M. met me with an imposing car at the station and took me to a grand house high in Bakewell. It was a strange family which was to produce some distinguished sons, but the chief thing about Mr M. was a passion for budgerigars. He had cages round the room, and would let the birds out at mealtimes to whirr around.

On the Sunday morning I was taken on a tour of the county, with its hills and stone walls, because Mrs M. wanted me to appreciate it. It was unhomely in a way to a native of the Thames Valley, but it taught me things that I had never thought of before. The cutting of stone for instance. Mr M. was an encyclopaedia on this. We stopped and he showed me buildings and the way stone had to be cut in special ways for different purposes, and how skilful cutting made stone weather better.

In between his talks Mrs M. wanted to interest me in Derbyshire history. Had I heard of Eyam? We would go there. Eyam was the heroic village of the Great Plague of 1655. London was devastated but nobody troubled about infection and a bundle of tailor's clothes was sent up to Eyam and plague broke out in the village. To stop a further spread the heroic villagers isolated themselves. People were forbidden to go or come, and dishes for food were put outside the boundaries. So the rest of Derbyshire escaped.

But Mrs M. had more than well-known stories. She had tales of the talk of old country people and the way that history lingered on in remote places. She talked of one old countryman who commented, 'That Anne Bullen was a rare quean. She did lead King Harry a dance.' The Boleyns had property nearby, Mrs M. said, so that mention of the family was not surprising. But he had used the old pronunciation of the name and the old word 'quean' for a light woman. When she had asked him where he had heard of Anne 'Bullen' he said that his grandfather had talked about her. He thought she had lived in Victorian times.

Ghosts, too, came into Mrs M.'s stories. She had met them herself. In the Great War, when her husband was in the army and she had three young children, she had rented an ancient Derbyshire farmhouse. She was warned that the house was haunted but she paid no attention. One night there was a tremendous knocking at the door, and she went and opened it, but there was nobody there. The knocking returned on other nights – so often that the family took no more notice of it.

Several times I visited the curiously congenial Mrs M., but my travels were usually to the south of Birmingham – the area of Stratford and the Cotswolds, which seemed the natural recreation region for Birmingham's more prosperous citizens who spent their leisure trying to get away from the town. Among callers at my office was a Mrs H., dark, a little mannered and very affable. She wrote articles in a cultivated hand and with convoluted grammar. I always remembered her sentence, 'Newly born, she went to see her grandson.' But she liked history and so did I.

She lived in the noted village of Chipping Campden, once the home of wool merchants. Now it was known for its golden-brown architecture and the arts and crafts which had been introduced by Charles Ashbee when he moved with his guild there in 1902.

Mrs H., widow of a Birmingham businessman, was an example of the cultivation I found in many Midland business families. She too invited me to visit her, and as usual I became a pupil rather than an editor.

Since leaving Cambridge I had suffered, I think, from commercialism and what I called 'the low-brows'. In journalism one could not expect people to be interested in Dante or Racine. But Mrs H. was a person of extreme refinement. Her low-ceilinged rooms had long bookshelves, and the curtains had a Burne-Jones design and there were Morris wallpapers. The local people were putting on plays, and in the evening Mrs H. took me out to see the barn where the performances were held.

Birmingham at the time was priding itself on being 'the city of a thousand trades' without bothering to ask about aesthetic values. Here was a contrast – the cult of handicrafts, tradition, rich textures. It was like returning to a university world . . .

But one visit to the Cotswolds, also to cultured women, ended unfortunately with anger in the villagers. This time it was to Willersey, then a small idyllic village, leading to the billowy Cotswold slopes. On the Sunday morning my hosts took me for a walk, and one of the things that, unexpectedly, interested me most was a view of rural poverty.

For years there had been a cult of a Garden-of-Eden countryside. Artists such as Birket Foster and Helen Allingham had, in Victorian times, excelled at views of thatched cottages, flowery gardens, mothers, with sunbonnets and babies, standing at wicket gates. Popular calendars had picked up the garden scenes of hollyhocks and roses. Children's books had stories of delicate children rescued from slums and growing healthy in pure air and a gardener's cottage. Later historians would put this rural idealism down to an attempt to escape from the growing squalor of cities.

During our morning walk from Willersey we followed a path across a field and came on a dilapidated structure without a garden or road. Pale thin barefoot children in shabby faded garments stood in front watching us, and there seemed to be no piped water or electricity. My companions said that this was a problem family living in poverty and primitive deprivation.

I had been shocked at living conditions in Birmingham's Summer Lane, but this country family seemed to be in a worse plight. I thought this over as I returned and, because journalists who can write what they like use their day-to-day experiences, I published an article on the problem family.

I had already written articles on the Summer Lane people, and they had known nothing about it. Willersey, in any case, had seemed far beyond the bounds of Birmingham. I had not had the slightest idea that these Cotswold people were seeing the Daily, but somebody in the neighbourhood did. The Willersey people were very angry, considering the article, I suppose, an aspersion on the neighbourhood.

'They've threatened to duck you in the village pond if you come again,' my friends said a little grimly. I could only apologise and try to be more careful another time. These were the days when journalists were not so merciless in breaking in on privacy.

No rash articles disturbed the days I spent with Mr E.W.J., who lived in a large old house near Alcester. From almost the beginning he had been sending me neatly-typed plain articles about 'nature' in the Warwickshire countryside. I had not liked them much, unreasonably reacting against their neatness. Then the author came to see me and turned out to be unexpectedly pleasant – a middle-aged bachelor living in the country and giving music lessons. It was not long before he too invited me to spend the day with him.

Mr E.W.J.'s house and garden stood on a high bank above a narrow road. In spring, I was told, it attracted sight-seers from miles around, for the bank was covered with a golden cloud of daffodils and narcissi. I saw it once towards the end of its splendour, and it was a sight never to be forgotten. In those days, anyhow, though bulbs were so cheap, there was not the habit of making spring displays in almost every garden and on many country banks.

Apart from the daffodils, I found, as I was to find in other Midland properties, almost a return to the eighteenth or nineteenth century. The house had large, chilly, lofty rooms, and in passages up and down stairs were stuffed birds and small animals in glass cases. The old housekeeper had a cupboard of her country wines and offered me dandelion, cowslip and turnip. Mr E.W.J., in rough country clothes and boots, conducted me round his large garden and discoursed on the weather and plants. On one occasion he took me out to see him cut some purple broccoli that he had been keeping for my lunch. Moles were making mounds in his lawn, and he talked of them with a mixture of interested naturalist and suffering gardener.

After a lunch of home-grown vegetables and fruit pie he took me for a walk to a hill from which, he said, you could see four counties. As he went he described butterflies that laid their eggs on the abundant nettles and the huge shiny black or dark brown slugs that after rain lurked in the long wayside grass. From the hill one could see clusters of trees which, he pointed out, included a number of pear trees. They abounded in Warwickshire because the wood had been used for furniture in the eighteenth century.

Sometimes he talked of the Romans, who had had a large camp at Alcester. It was many years before this was to be scientifically excavated, but E.W.J. said that people were constantly finding relics – bits of pottery or coins. He reported on one occasion that a village friend had just dug up a Roman coin in his garden. The public in those days had little of today's excited interest in archaeology, and metal detectors would have been thought a scientific impossibility.

Mr E.W.J. was also interested in modern arts. He asked me if I had heard of a composer named Britain or Britten, and he talked about literary figures who, with the increase of cars, were coming to live in the area. One was John Moore, who in the 'thirties wrote immensely popular books on the countryside. On another of my visits he mentioned a project to build a village hall. Farms round were still only half mechanised, and many agricultural workers still populated the villages.

When, laden with fruit and vegetables, I returned to Birmingham on a narrow railway track through woods, I was depressed as usual at the dirty brick. However, I was to find quite soon that there were green oases in the city desert. Another countryman began to entertain me within five miles of the city centre.

Soon after my arrival Geo. W. told me that he had found a man to do weekly gardening notes for the women's page. He considered gardening very much a lady's occupation.

The writer was to be Mr W., the chief gardener at The Grove, the large Harborne property near Geo. W.'s own Harborne house. I was not pleased. I wanted literary not practical stuff. But 'he'll come and make arrangements with you,' the editor said with his agreeable habit of leaving responsibility to us. So I waited rather discontentedly.

A few days later a broad-shouldered man knocked on my office door. He had a brick-brown face, very blue eyes and curly, iron-grey hair, and he spoke with a charming country accent – Gloucestershire perhaps. He was nervous and very anxious to be obliging, and in a few minutes anybody would have been his friend.

After that his notes were delivered regularly every Friday evening – in time for the Saturday paper and weekend gardening. He wrote in a round uncultivated hand, giving practical instructions about regular sowings and plantings that he was doing himself. It was before the days of TV dissertations on rare plants with long names, but he did have care of some glasshouses so that his notes were fairly wide-ranging and included delicate pot plants.

Then the usual thing happened – an invitation to spend the afternoon in 'his' garden. So one day I travelled to Harborne that in some parts remained countrified, and found some large gates.

Mr W. was standing there waiting for me, with brown bare arms and his gardening apron. I went there a number of times at different seasons and was given a tour of greenhouses, providing carnations and other flowers for entertainments at the big house, and the vegetable garden with its neat green rows. The tour ended near Mr W.'s own cottage, where he had three or four beehives, and I found him an excellent talker on bee management.

He spoke of honey extraction, hive control, feeding bees in winter and catching swarms. Some of his methods seemed pretty heartless to my girlish romanticism – that of killing off colonies deliberately.

But, Mr W. said, individual bees in summer live for only a few weeks anyhow. He mixed practical measures with a paternal affection, and he told me stories of bee intelligence and self-sacrifice.

One story was of a wasp invasion. He noticed a crowd of wasps determinedly crawling up the entrance to a hive. They were trying to raid it for honey, but the guardian bees resisted them. The guardian bees were stung to death, but more and more bees emerged to fight. The battle went on for hours, and finally, Mr W. said, there were dead bees scattered all round the hive, but the wasps were dead too.

After looking at the hives we went in to tea at the cottage. Mrs W. was waiting – roly-poly, nervous, smiling and kind, with fluttering eyelashes and another country accent. She gave me a good tea, and afterwards Mr W. conducted me back to the big gates and I caught a bus to the office.

Through the years I grew fond of the W.s who were so obliging and so unfailing in the gardening notes. But people never stick to type, and after a time Mr W.'s broad figure, which had been a picture of country health, sagged and his face grew a little haggard. He told me that he had had indigestion, and the doctor 'says I smoke too much'. He had got into the habit of going round the gardens all day with a cigarette in his mouth. We did not know then that smoking was bad for you, but we had a vague idea that one could overdo it. The doctor told Mr W. to 'cut it down', and he came to see me and said he had given up smoking and felt much better.

Another unexpected thing about the W.s was that they had a son who was a journalist. Presently the notes arrived neatly typed, and so they continued till the war, when the women's page ended. Neither of the parent W.s had very long lives.

Towards the end of the period I met the owner of the estate, who came of the well-known Nettlefold family. She asked me to tea, and I went to The Grove's big house instead of the cottage. We had polite conversation, and I mentioned the W.s. The lady treated them with a trace of condescension, recalling that, when their cottage was being modernised, they were shocked at the idea of having a lavatory inside a house. 'You see, they had always been used to a toilet down the garden path.'

Well, that only showed what country people they were. They were part of Birmingham's great variety.

Finally The Grove became a public park.

Christmas

In the middle of my first autumn Mr G., the literary editor, pushed into my room with a pile of brightly coloured shiny books which he dumped on the floor. 'By the beginning of December,' he said.

The Daily devoted two of its large pages to Christmas books. The columns had small headings, long paragraphs and no signatures in the paper's old-fashioned way of keeping as much as possibly anonymous. The pages looked dull, but presumably the publishers read it as they provided some advertisements. The book notes were divided – young children's books, boys' books, girls' books and adults' books. I was given the girls'.

After this, in autumns up to the war, I had this shiny autumn pile stacked in my room. The operation always followed the same pattern. Mr G. would arrive soon after I had returned from my annual holiday, at a time when Christmas seemed months ahead. Being busy, I would leave the books unregarded in a corner. Then, in November, I would realise that there were only a few weeks left for me to read the stuff – always the longest part of reviewing – and would decide that I must come in and work on a Saturday afternoon.

In a way I looked forward to those solitary afternoons with highwaymen and Doris of the Fifth. Through the wet cold streets I would walk from the bus and call in at a café for some solid cakes. Shopping crowds would be milling about, and the newsmen would be bawling with their sports papers. But I would leave all this commotion and turn up the narrow street to the Daily's side entrance.

The watchman would wish me the usual friendly good afternoon, and I would climb the stairs and feel the warmth of the office. By the landing with the large sea picture all would be silent except for the loudly ticking clock. I would switch on my light and fire, gather half a dozen books and sink into my soft armchair. At times I would hear a step or a shout far off, with the faint rumble of machinery as the evening paper was published. The watchman, doing his rounds and seeing my light, would peer in, but otherwise I was undisturbed.

The books, with coloured paper jackets, several illustrations and perhaps a coloured frontispiece, would cost from 1s. 6d. to 5s. Some of them still dealt with emotional entanglements at boarding schools in the manner of the Angela Brazils of earlier in the century. I remember nothing of more plebeian day schools which were to occupy story writers later. But the boarding school epics might now be given a foreign flavour, no doubt after the author's summer trip abroad – with a few bonjours and Grüss-Gotts. The heroine generally had a hard time at first, was despised by her fellows or thought to be a thief, but ended triumphantly, often proving a great actress in a school play. The mistresses, as far as I remember, were goddess-like and benevolent.

There were plenty of historical stories but they were of the most obvious periods – the Elizabethans, the French Revolution, high-waymen and smugglers. Prehistoric or Ancient British children were yet to come, and the girls' authors of the 'thirties did not, I think, do the careful research done by later writers.

There was some magic after the style of E. Nesbit, but this was generally in books for younger children. Almost all the volumes bestowed on me by Mr G. contained stories. The lavishly illustrated books of information, the enthusiasm for birds and ecology (then known at 'nature'), had not arrived. But the writing was probably better than today's, with fewer grammar mistakes and less American slang. When violence was mentioned it was brief, and the author did not dwell on horrors, and love intruded in a romantic devotional way. The books were for a more innocent generation.

But the trouble with these stories on those drowsy Saturday afternoons was that they were too interesting. I would expect to gallop through half a dozen volumes but find that by seven I had read only two. I would decide that I should have to come back on another Saturday afternoon.

I spent hours in reading, and in the end wrote only a few clotted hundred words. When I had delivered my notes to Mr G., he would send a boy down to carry away the books, which would be sent to a local hospital. The book pages appeared in the middle of the week when the paper was otherwise comparatively small, and they looked to me too crammed ever to be read by the public. Then they were forgotten. Books were still given largely as presents in those days, but how much the Daily's notes affected givers was unknown.

After a few years a huge new Christmas job appeared for me. It was to become an endurance test but, like the book pages, it was probably a waste of time.

The idea came from Wag, who was still trying to brighten the paper and stimulate advertisements. There were consultations with the advertising manager and then the idea was put to me. What about a Christmas shopping supplement?

The advertising department was to woo local shops to 'take space'. Advertisements as usual were to line the sides of the pages. In the middle were to appear Christmas pictures, and I was to visit the shops and supply the text. We began with two pages but through the years they increased to six.

It was easy for George the photographer. All he had to do was to wander round and find some children with their noses glued to a shop window or a toddler sitting on the knee of one of the Father Christmases at the larger stores. But I had to tramp round all the shops, writing with delight about corkscrews decorated with dogs' heads or stagecoach calendars.

The Daily generally went into contortions to avoid mentioning trade names, but now this rule was relaxed. I had to mention the name of the firm and be pleased with everything. Each year I began energetically, rising in the dim late morning and going straight into town. But after about four shops and conversations and note-taking I would begin to flag, and retire to the office and evening work as to a haven of rest.

Toy shops were among the easiest subjects, especially those with educational or foreign toys. The great age of education through play had not arrived, nor had plastics, but there were brightly coloured or natural coloured solid wooden trains and wagons, often from Scandinavia. Other shops were more difficult.

In the big stores what department did one choose, and what exactly counted as a Christmas present? Hot water bottles, rugs, egg cups? It was easier if there was a Santa Claus or elves' cave. One could describe them at length and leave the rest vague. But only one or two Birmingham stores provided such entertainment. In large shops I was often conducted from one department to another and received pages of information that I could not use or, as a contrast, would be informed that Mr X, for whom I had been told to talk, was busy and could I come back?

Tobacconists and wine-sellers were difficult. They had so small a range and I knew so little of their products that I used sometimes to fall back on describing their decorations. Sometimes I came across products that I really liked – heavy Swedish glass, or milky Lalique glass decorated by one chaste fish or leaf, or Finnish furniture in pale woods. But my independent judgment told me that most of the Christmas 'lines' were gimcrackery. In the 'thirties, suburban mantelpieces still had rows of ornaments – vases with orange and green decorations, small mirrors decorated with pink roses, pottery rabbits and dogs. Crinoline ladies were everywhere – on pincushions, tea cosies, tablecloths, crockery.

There were frilly covers, surely difficult to wash, to keep boiled eggs warm, and nightdress cases embroidered with dogs' heads. The metal ware was endless – paper knives shaped like swords, fancy teaspoons and tin trays with pictures of thatched cottages, ships at sea or ladies semi-nude with snake locks. One year hearth furniture – pokers with dog's heads – was said to be the Christmas 'thing'. The stationery shop I visited had framed prints in bright colours, with bluebell woods, hunting scenes and stage coaches as favourites. Ashtrays in several materials with decorations of Stratford-upon-Avon or cats were everywhere.

The shopkeepers were keen to stress local talent. 'All made in Birmingham,' they would say proudly at a display of knickknacks, and I would be torn between admiration at Birmingham industry and uneasiness at its lack of taste. But then, of course, the average shopper had no taste either. So I dilated on Birmingham's products.

I wrote my pieces without the gushing adjectives of women's journalism, and the chunks of description were probably dull. At the end another woman journalist friend gave me a little help, but it was a time of desperate typing, proof-reading and page-arrangement. On the evening before the supplement appeared the rest of the paper would be kept small. 'Viss is your night,' Wag would say on his evening visit, and I would go up early to the composing room for the last stages of marking misprints, cutting bits out to make the 'stories' fit and then rereading. When it was over I felt as if I had been through an examination.

When I reached home at 1.00 a.m. I would put on my gas fire and spread the paper on the floor in front of it, glance through the pages and read here and there. Perhaps they did not read so badly, but the trite Birmingham-glorifying headings would have seemed comic to anybody outside the area. People, I thought, might look at George's pretty Christmas pictures in the centre of the pages and at the advertisements along the edges, but no-one could possibly wade through all those columns of print.

Perhaps some did. Perhaps people read about the shops that they frequented. The shopkeepers themselves must have read the stuff, for some of them sent messages of thanks. But no doubt my labour went largely unread, and in any case, in a day or two, the subject was as defunct as ancient Egypt. The passing of Christmas itself kills all Christmas subjects dead. Journalism is a great waste of time.

Cars

''Ere, you ought to get a car of your own,' Wag said to me one evening in the composing room.

The idea seemed quite good. I could take out some of my Summer Lane acquaintances and show them the countryside that they had never seen. I could motor home to my family. I could go on motoring holidays.

It was all very easy. There were no driving tests and almost no rules of the road. Petrol was a shilling a gallon. Pimmy, my kind printer, said he knew a neighbour who dealt in second-hand cars.

The neighbour found one quite soon. It was a Morris of the old 1925 type which had a round nose. It cost fifty pounds, but the neighbour said it was roadworthy. There were, of course, no MOT tests in those days. It would not go at more than thirty miles an hour, but that did not matter at a time when you could choose your own pace on the comparatively empty roads.

I was to leave the Morris with Pimmy until I found a local garage. Somebody told me that a sweet factory near my flat had a yard with sheds for cars. I visited the place and found a yard edged with somewhat tumbledown buildings. Heaven knows what kinds of sweets the place produced, but a strong smell of acid drops hung in the air. One of the sheds was empty, and the owner said I could have half of it for half-a-crown a week. The place seemed damp, but I had the impression that cars were sturdy things and could stand a bit of moisture.

Pimmy's neighbour, a youngish obliging man, who had found the car, said he would give me driving lessons. I went out to Yardley and found the car, which looked huge to me. I got in and he told me how to start and use the gears and brake; and we bumped along ruts in the lanes, and I felt like a lone pea in a pod. The Morris made a great deal of noise, but I had no idea how much noise a car ought to make.

After two outings with the neighbour I said I was going to drive home to Surrey, about 120 miles. The neighbour was mildly disapproving. 'If you was my daughter I shouldn't let you go,' he said, but neither he nor Pimmy, who knew little of cars, seemed to think there was any danger. The roads were fairly empty, and there was little about road accidents in the papers. The great volume of road legislation was not yet in sight. And after all I did know how to start, change gears and put on the brakes, though the Morris ones were not very good.

'Well, if you must go, take it gently,' the neighbour said.

I picked up the car at Yardley on a Saturday morning in one of my home weekends. Pimmy had looked up the places I should go through. It was spring, and there was plenty of time before the evening. So I rattled cheerfully through Birmingham till I came to a road island with a large vehicle in the way. To be rid of it I turned to the right and went round the island that side.

Fortunately nothing was coming in the other direction, but a policeman saw and stopped me. I explained that I was only just learning to drive ad was trying to get to Surrey, and he was quite pleasant. 'Well, don't do it again,' he said, and let me go. A long time later I reached Warwick, and then, after what seemed hours, Banbury. It was comparatively easy rattling along the empty roads, though the miles seemed longer than they had done when I was in other people's cars. It was when I reached the towns, I found, that the difficulties came. There was traffic about, and the signposts were few and small. You passed them so quickly that you could hardly read them.

Presently I found myself heading from Banbury to Northampton, which was not the way I wanted to go. I drove on for some minutes hoping that somehow, by a miracle, the road would turn out really to be going to London; but still it went east towards Northampton. In the end, when I was almost in the country again, I decided to turn back, and I made my first attempts to turn the car. But the car was large and the road narrow, and I sawed backwards and forwards for some time, holding up other cars and getting angry glances. However, in the end I did get round and turned again to Banbury.

The hours passed, and still I was only about half way. Oxford, round which I had previously wandered in a poetic mood, thinking of Matthew Arnold and Gerard Manley Hopkins, became a menacing kaleidoscope of traffic, and I was sweating with fear when I left it. Then there were twenty lonely miles to Henley-on-Thames. Just outside Henley I must have been nearly killed, for on a long straight road I saw a car rushing towards me, and somehow I could not get my Morris enough to the left. We seemed to fly down the centre of the road in nightmare helplessness, and then the car was on me with a blast and what seemed half an inch to spare. It rushed by me, and again I was in a sweat of terror. But, yes, I was still alive.

The afternoon was passing. I toiled up and down on the way to hilly Maidenhead, and then came the flat lands of the Windsor area. I got lost again, and now the traffic was increasing as I came nearer to London. After driving for hours through the empty countryside I felt I could not adjust to traffic; yet I never thought of stopping and resting for a moment. On I went with more narrow escapes, and passed through Staines, with a wickedly difficult right-hand turn, to Kingston. Then in the distance I saw something that I knew – Hampton Court Palace. It seemed incredible that I could reach it by road all the way from Birmingham.

When at last I drove in at the home gate I had been for more than seven hours on the road – covering 120 miles. I was so stiff I could hardly move. My family strayed out, admired the car and did not think I had done anything very difficult. I wanted sympathy, but they knew as little about cars as I did.

All that night I was driving the Morris, rushing by other cars, switching round corners, getting lost. In the morning I was jaded and still terrified; and I should have to drive back on Monday.

I did drive back – in about six hours.

Accidents

I did a good deal with my old cars of the 1930s, taking many people out and having touring holidays. But when I look back on my motoring I remember chiefly the worries and terrors.

They began at the sweet-factory shed where I garaged the Morris and the old Fiat that followed it. The shed lost its door and grew damper as the years went by, and, as I used the car nearly always at weekends only, there was plenty of time for it to degenerate. Sometimes I would find cats' paw marks all over the bonnet, and things seemed often to go wrong. A tyre was flat or the battery had failed, and often the car would not start. I had to try to swing the front handle, which needed both strength and knack. Sometimes the pale-haired four-year-old son of the proprietor would come and watch my efforts, and very occasionally one of the men about the yard would swing the handle for me.

Sometimes when I was out I had to get the car to start by pushing it. I took this to be normal with cars. Beside making a hideous noise, the Morris gave a deafening series of pistol shots with its exhaust when I descended after climbing a hill, and its floorboard behind jumped about as I rattled along. Once, when the board had jerked right out, I lost a fine new motoring rug, a gift, through the hole in the floor.

People said it was normal for a new driver to have a few accidents. The trouble was that I knew nothing of the way cars worked, and I had no tools. At the same time there were dark stories of the immoral practices of garages in this ever-increasing field of trade with many ignorant drivers. The garages, it was said, overcharged, and some of them, in putting things right, put something else wrong so that you had to come back. Their work was also casual and slipshod, and they answered to nobody. I had at least one experience of this.

I was always vaguely worried that I should not get my passengers back safely. Once I had taken an old Summer Lane lady and her family to Broadway in the Cotswolds, and I thought I would drive them up the steep Fish Hill to show them the view. They had never been in a car before so when, half way up the hill, the engine stuttered and stopped they were not perturbed. I had not the slightest idea what was wrong, but I had to put the brake on hard as we were a heavy load on a steep slope. With a feeling of panic I fiddled about, and suddenly the engine started again – again I did not know why. So we got to the top of the hill and back and I was in Birmingham in time for the evening's work.

I took all this as normal, though I was amazed one summer when I travelled with a friend's new car in Scotland at how easy it was to drive. I never thought of buying a new car myself. I had other things to do with my money. Instead I complained that an afternoon out with a family could be very expensive. When I took out a party of, say, five and gave them tea, petrol and café could cost as much as ten shillings, now fifty pence.

Once on the long road between Oxford and Henley I smelt the sickening odour of burning rubber and saw clouds of smoke rising from the bonnet. There was nobody about, and I had not the faintest idea what to do beyond turning off the engine. Then I had luck, for an AA man came along and stopped. He was very good and patched up my connections.

I had two comparatively bad accidents. One was again on that empty Oxford-Henley road, when you went on mile after mile as if you were in a dream. I came over a humped bridge, and a bicycle shot out from the left across my path. I swerved right and hit a wall and grazed the bicycle. A stout girl fell off, and her leg began to bleed badly. When I took her in at the big gates from which she had sped I found it was a mental hospital; but I think she was a maid and not a patient. The hospital people were kind and bound up her leg. Her story was that I had appeared over the hump suddenly without warning. I was surprised that she had not heard the Morris.

But the hospital people must have thought that she was in the wrong, for they merely took my name and address and let me go. I walked out to find the car bonnet against the wall, the windscreen in fragments with scattered glass on the road and the car itself knocked crooked. I crawled away on the long journey home in a howling gale without the windscreen, and I had to steer sharply right all the time to keep the car straight. It took me even more hours than usual to get home, and the man at the local garage seemed surprised that I could drive it at all. I had to leave the car there and go back by train. But I heard no more from the Oxfordshire mental hospital.

The other accident might also have ended in death. I was touring with my mother in Somerset when I noticed that the car pulled to the left. Always in fear of some calamity, I trundled it into a smart Minehead garage full of elegant holiday cars. I was grateful that the attendant did not show scorn but told me to call the next day and he would have the car ready. So I called, and he assured me that the trouble was the brake, and that had been corrected. I paid and we started out light-heartedly to climb the celebrated Porlock Hill. Luckily, knowing the car's habit of breaking down, I took the slightly less steep toll road.

We had, however, a sheer drop on our right, and when the car lurched suddenly and went loose I was glad that we were a few feet from the edge. I could do nothing with it; it was like trying to push along something with a broken back. So I went to the RAC man at the top of the hill and asked him to have a look.

He came obligingly, took a look and said in horror, 'You haven't driven up the hill with *that*?' The collapse was because the axle rod had broken. A crack had been the cause of the pull to the left, and tightening the brake had caused the complete fracture. 'You're lucky to be alive,' the RAC man said. Yes, it *was* a terrible thing to happen, and the repair would be long and expensive.

'But,' I protested, 'it's just been in a garage.'

'Ah,' he said. 'They knew you were touring and wouldn't come back. Garages in holiday places are like that.'

The car had to be towed down to Porlock, and we had to wait for some days while the axle rod was welded. The bill added a good deal to our holiday expenses.

Presently I changed my old Morris for an equally old Fiat, which was said to be good on hills but was very slow. It did not seem much of an improvement, but I was not looking for anything grand and I relied on Pimmy's neighbour who had found me the first car. The Fiat did not have any accidents, but almost every vehicle on the road passed it.

I had no sense of guilt at rattling round in old crocks. Other people were doing it, and the problems of too many cars, of road accidents and exhaust fumes were far in the future. But I did begin to hate going round to the sweet factory after, say, a week of rain and finding yet another mishap.

I longed for an adviser who would know something about cars' insides, but at that time there was nobody near me. Then the war came, and pleasure motoring ended, and I was glad in a way.

Pimmy, always kind, said he would ask the neighbour to dispose of the car for me. It went finally – for a pound.

Moving Out

In the 'thirties Birmingham Corporation began to build new estates and move people out from the central poor streets. I was toiling round Summer Lane and many times had heard the cry, 'If only we could get out of here . . .'

So I was delighted one afternoon when Mrs C., who lived in a side street off Summer Lane, stood by her door which opened straight on to the street and said with a beaming smile, 'We'm going to be moved at last.'

I had liked Mrs C. from the early days when I used to see her with an older Mrs C. This was the mother-in-law who was living with the family of husband and wife and two boys in a house of one bedroom and an attic. The two women seemed on the best of terms, and the younger Mrs C. nursed the older one when she got ill and died.

Mrs C. junior was a frail dark woman with looped-up hair and a glass eye. She told me that she had lost her eye in some maternity trouble, but I did not know what. She had a soft confiding voice, smiled frequently and told me her troubles. Mr C. had some poor labouring job, but he had kept it in the Slump, and Mrs C. saved threepence a week, a respectable sum, with the 'Provident'.

The two sons were thin but clean with their hair closely cropped. Billy was eight when I first called and Johnnie five. Billy was undersized but had some colour in his cheeks and was said to be doing well at school. Johnnie was a wispy little boy with a red nose, and he had suffered from a series of disasters. He had had pneumonia, Mrs C. told me, four times and had also been run over in the horse road.

Soon after I began to visit her, Mrs C. was in great distress. Johnnie was being transferred from his infants' school to a special school because he was considered mentally subnormal. 'It's only because of them illnesses,' she said to me, and she went up the infants' school to protest. But it was no good. The machine had moved on and the case had been decided. And then, in a way, it seemed not such a bad thing after all. Johnnie was taken from one of the dreary schools of the Summer Lane area and put in a school which dealt with children from a wide area and had extra money devoted to it. Johnnie would stay there till he was sixteen, two years longer than most children. Mrs C. went up to see it and came back saying it was nice and bright.

The boys had never seen the country, and I took them out in my old car. I remember how they stood among long grass in a meadow, not quite knowing what to do. Then I arranged a week's holiday for Mrs C. and the boys at Malvern. When I went to call for them they were brown and said they had had a good time, but I had the impression that they had not enjoyed themselves as much as suburban children might have done. They were not geared to rural things. They knew nothing of wild life. But they had got on well with the landlady and she had told them about her family, and they had been for some nice walks.

We continued in contact and the boys became gawky lads. Mrs C.'s worries grew. Her house faced on to the street. There was not even a court to retire to. And she said there were terrible lads in the street, and she was afraid that 'our Billy' would go with them and get into trouble with the police. 'But how can I keep the boys in?' she said. 'There's only the kitchen to sit in.' Again and again she repeated, 'If we could only get out of this.'

Then one afternoon she greeted me with a wide smile. The street had been condemned, and the Council was moving all the people out. The family was to be taken to see its new dwelling – a house on a corner at Kingstanding, one of Birmingham's first planned estates.

The house had a larger garden than most and a bathroom. Billy would get away from the bad boys and Johnnie would have fresh air.

We should have to part, of course. There would be no 'Provident' there. But I would go out to see them. It seemed as if the family was really on the upward path.

But then, a week after their move, I ran into Mrs C., to my astonishment, near to Summer Lane. She was her old worried self. She said she had come into town to shop. It cost her a shilling here and back on the bus, but what shops there were on the estate were dreadfully expensive, standoffish and a long way away. She knew the old cheap places round the Lane. 'So I just take a bus and come in,' she said.

But a shilling for fares was a great deal in those days. 'I don't know how we're going to manage, I'm sure,' she added. Then there was her husband too. In moving the family out the Council had made problems for Mr C. who had a job in the centre of town. He had terribly big bus fares now, and he had to get up an hour earlier to be at work in time.

As for the boys, the move had not made much difference to Johnnie, who was always taken to school by special bus. But her fears for Billy were greater than ever. To prevent the new residents from being lonely the Council had moved all the people of the street together, so that the bad boys were still about. Billy had been accepted by a local school, but it had 'an awful lot of rough lads'. Mrs C. finished with the old lament: 'I don't know what we shall do, I'm sure.'

But if things do not turn out as well as you expect, they may not be as bad as you feared. I went out to see the family and remember my first view of the estate as I got down from the bus. There was a very wide road with the wind blowing along it, and up hill and down dale were hundreds of small houses, alike and monotonous. It was a desert in its way, but at least there was plenty of air.

I visited without previous notice as I was not sure if Mrs C. could read letters, but, when I found the right corner house and banged on the door, I had a pleasant surprise. The kitchen was fairly large, clean and cheerful, and Mrs C. showed me round the house with a little pride. There were three small bedrooms and a bathroom that was clean. It disproved the silly story going the rounds that, when back-street families were moved to new houses, they kept their coals in the bath. Later a social worker told me that this was a complete fiction.

Outside there was a good stretch of rough ground for a garden, and Mr C. said her husband was digging it when he had time. But he got home later than in the old days because of the long journey. She herself was lonely. 'Sometimes I don't see nobody all day,' she said. And the boys? Well, Billy was not very happy at the new school. It had so many wild lads who had moved out from the town. But Johnnie was always contented, even though the school bus had to call for him earlier and he had a long day.

Anyhow the move was over, and the C.s had not tried to return. I went out several times to see the family. The good news was that Johnnie's breathing was better, but quite unexpectedly the bad news was the degeneration of the good elder boy, Billy. He had two troubles. Bad boys were about on the estate, and there was even less for boys to do there than in the city. At that time it had hardly been realised that it is not enough just to give people housing. They need shopping centres, places of entertainment and clubs. The Corporation had appointed a social worker to help the families to settle down, but there was simply not enough, except for gardening, for them to do in their spare time. Local authorities have learnt a great deal about social welfare since then.

Billy's second problem was adolescence. He reacted badly to that disturbed period of life. He left school at fourteen and got a job, but did not keep it, nor several other jobs that followed. I was shocked when I saw him. He had shot up to be taller than his father, and was unshaven and shaggy. He seemed to keep no job more than a fortnight, and he had begun to smoke heavily.

Later his behaviour became even worse. He refused to work at all, and of course paid nothing for his keep. He stayed in bed for half the day, and when he got up coaxed his mother to give him money for cigarettes. His father, though he was smaller than Billy, beat him, Mrs C. said. Then Billy threatened to hit back. Now he went out when his father came in.

Luckily it was before the time of drug peddling. But still Mrs C. was full of fears. Billy might break in somewhere as he needed so much money for smoking. Or he might injure his father in a quarrel. But now another unexpected thing happened. The feeble Johnnie became important. His special school had trained him well, and he was better in health. He got a job when he left school at sixteen, kept it and brought all his money to his mother. Billy, who now had no friends, reacted by hardly speaking to his younger brother, but with Johnnie's help the family's money worries were a little lightened.

The story of the C.s, as I last heard it, did not end too badly. Billy finally 'listed as a sojer' and presumably was rehabilitated. Johnnie kept his job and remained his mother's pride. The family grew used to the estate and improved in health. Then the war came and stopped my visits.

I know of other people who were moved out from the Summer Lane area, and families looking up in the world moved on their own initiative. If they did not come back in the first few weeks they did not come back at all. Presently more amenities were provided on the new estates. The chief trouble now was that all those small red houses ate up miles and miles of countryside.

The tower blocks seemed at one time a solution to this problem. I was not there to hear what desolation they inflicted on back-street communities in the Midlands.

Change

At every New Year the Daily printers went through a shattering ritual. As midnight of December 31 began to strike they stopped work, seized the nearest thing that would make a noise – bell, whistle, rattle, mallet, piece of metal – and raised so terrific a din that people said it could be heard as far off as Chamberlain Square at the end of New Street. You could certainly hear it all over our rambling building, even through closed doors and windows.

On my first New Year's Eve, after I had been in Birmingham for nearly a year, the printers invited me to the composing room to hear the noise. I accepted, not knowing what was going to happen, and then was frozen with shock. When the noise began I thought I should be deafened for life. One was aware not only of the unbearable racket but of the twanging of air waves past one's ears. It was hell. I kept away from the ceremony in future.

But the ceremony and the years went on. I had told myself when I came to Birmingham that I would not stay more than two years, but the two years went by and I was deep in contacts and jobs. And presently it became home and most of my friends were there.

The office changed little for a time, and it remained warm physically and emotionally. Some old people went, and there were collections for presents and rather embarrassing ceremonies. Some new reporters came. Spotty office boys, following on the heels of old

Jack, changed several times. The greatest shock was the sudden death of the dramatic critic R.C.R., with whom I had gone out to Stratford. But another dramatic critic was appointed, and life went on.

Then something was whispered which brought a breath of insecurity. Geo. W. was to retire. He had been with the Birmingham papers for thirty years, coming as a reporter to the evening 'Mail', rising to be its editor and then being promoted to the Daily. His habits – the chain-smoking with the long cigarette-holder, the affluent car, the punctual departure at 10.10 each night – had become part of the office tradition. The leader writers with their Oxford degrees may have talked of him a little condescendingly, but had comfortable jobs with him.

'You'll never get to know the editor,' people had said when I arrived and, though he had invited me to his house and taken me out, I never felt easy with him. Yet in small troubles he had stood by me, and he was incorruptible in an old-fashioned way.

I always remembered how, at my first Christmas, a fashion house in London sent me a wristwatch. We had used plenty of its photographs during the year, and in any case it was probably sending out watches to other papers. But I did not want to be bribed, and I took the watch to Geo. W. 'You'd better send it back at once,' he said, and I did.

Now he was over sixty and would retire to Bournemouth, which in the 'thirties was the Mecca of Birmingham people. In spite of his position – or perhaps because of it – he did not seem to have made many friends in Birmingham. His son was dead. There was nothing to keep him.

If I had been sensible I should have expressed regrets at his departure. I had a great respect for him and I saw him almost daily. But I was too shy to say anything, and he said nothing either. Meanwhile a collection for a present went round the office, and we all gave more than usual. A clock, so often a retirement gift, was to be bought.

Then it was announced that the ceremony was to take place in his room early one evening. 'The old man will hate it,' somebody said. 'He can't bear making speeches.' All the same he had to bow to convention.

Early in the evening, before the rush to get the paper out, we were rounded up, quiet and embarrassed. Top people from the firm, a representative from every department, and men from the other papers in the group stood about in the large bare room. In the middle was a table piled with boxes.

People talked in low voices. Geo. W. and his editorial men stood in the centre. 'Well,' L.P.H., the deputy editor, said at last, 'I suppose we'd better begin.' So the speeches from heads of departments were made. Geo. W. was said to be 'the finest editor the paper has ever known,' and small jokes were made about his cars and his hatred of public speaking. Geo. W. himself, a spare figure with his clipped greying beard and balding head, stood enduring the praise but did not pretend to enjoy it.

The boxes were handed over. So much money had been sub-scribed that several presents had been bought including, I think, a cigarette-holder. Then Geo. W. had to express his thanks. 'Well,' he said, 'I detest speech-making,' and he did not make a speech; thanked everybody in a few sentences and wished the paper well. Nobody in any case could linger long, for the Daily had to be produced.

Afterwards the men crowded round shaking hands. I was the only woman there, and did not want to intrude. I lingered a moment, then wandered out, thinking I would return when the crowds had gone. But when I went back to the big room it was dark and empty. Geo. W. had not waited.

I ought to have written to him but did not. He had left that feeling of embarrassment behind. He moved to Bournemouth and dropped out of our lives.

But years later I had proof of his benevolence. A letter with his handwriting lay on my desk. I knew the even writing at once, and through old habit felt a jump of apprehension. But I need not have worried.

At the time I was producing articles on the effect of the war on Birmingham organisations. Out of the blue Geo. W. was writing to congratulate me. He found the articles 'very interesting'.

There was no earthly compulsion on him to write. There had been no contact for years. But I suppose he was still reading his Birmingham paper with care, and he had always been good to his staff.

This time I did write to him. I did not hear from him again, and he died soon afterwards.

New Boss

One thing I learnt about office life when Geo. W. retired: when a man is in a position of authority he is lauded up to the skies. His henchmen speak of him with reverence. But when he retires he becomes a nobody. He no longer is of any interest and is quickly forgotten. In offices there is little independent criterion of character; the position is everything. Perhaps women are less subservient than men; more independent in judgment. But generally an office combines to flatter the boss and afterwards forget him. This happened with our new editor.

For a time we did not know who it was to be. I saw the leader writers talking in low tones outside their rooms. They naturally hoped that somebody from the Birmingham office would be elevated. L.P.H., the deputy editor, had the best chance, but he was elderly and had been there for many years, writing leaders in his distinctive green ink in longhand on home affairs, and he was abrupt and often silent. Somebody more dynamic was needed for a paper whose circulation was still too small.

Later Mrs L.P.H. remarked that her husband had been abominably treated; but he, of course, said nothing. The news filtered through that a Mr R., who for some years had been in charge of the London office, was to join us as editor. And now everybody began to sing Mr R.'s praises. 'He's very jolly,' people said. Also he was being tremendously courageous to leave London where he had spent so many years, and settle in Birmingham.

Verging on sixty, he was an old-fashioned Liberal. The Daily, founded in Victorian times when the Chamberlains were growing in fame, had followed the Liberal Joseph Chamberlain who yet opposed Home Rule in Ireland. I was always to say 'Unionist' and not 'Conservative', I was told when I came to Birmingham, and the distinction was carefully preserved through the 'thirties, though it meant little. Mr R. was of the right breed.

He had been born in Warwickshire, and was interested in country things, including hunting. People hinted that he had had a struggle to survive in journalism. Whether that was true or not he had developed an enormous delight in titles and landed gentry, and he constantly introduced well-known people into his conversation. He was a bachelor like 'Charlie' and, I was to be told later, very much a woman-hater after some disappointment. He spent his money on precious things and cigars.

But always his 'jolliness' was stressed. I expected something very warm and genial on the evening when he arrived. Members of the staff were lined up outside the editor's room to greet him. He appeared, a broad-shouldered man with white hair and moustache, a square face, low blue eyes and rather small features. Vaguely, at the back of my mind, was the feeling that he was like a tabby cat.

He did not seem very jolly but more like a schoolmaster. He shook each of us firmly by the hand and said, 'I'll come and see you later.' Then we were dismissed.

Afterwards he strode into my room and asked me what I did for the paper. I did not then know of his dislike of women, but he had an air of command. I showed him a women's page which that night had more advertisements than usual so that there were only two articles and a few paragraphs. He said sternly, 'Is that all?' as if I were taking wages for doing nothing.

He was to make other people uncomfortable. A woman reviewer told me that he had sent her the rudest letter she had ever had in her life. He was a man of moods, and when he came in biting his moustache one knew that trouble was brewing. But he was also much swayed by outside opinion as Geo. W. was not, and when later he heard praise for the women's page he was pleased and told me so.

He also liked teasing. At least on one occasion he made me use a 'pretty' hunting picture when he knew that I hated hunting. This brought up the old problem of journalism. Should you insist on your principles or serve your newspaper in a neutral way? On this occasion I used the hunting picture. I did not see what else I could do. Later, however, he became more genial and when another photograph of a meet came up did not make me use it.

Mr R., having no family to occupy him, was in the office most of the day, as Geo. W. had not been, and the odour of his cigars was always about the place. His longer hours gave him a chance to interfere, and crises blew up more often than in the old days.

Newspaper production is always a rush against time, and Mr R. would storm if any page was late, as it might be because an advertisement or a wanted piece of news had not arrived. I always marvelled on these occasions at the way the men humoured him, not explaining but putting the blame on somebody else. Several times Wag, who was generally so much a friend, became a traitor.

The women's page was supposed to be finished by ten, before the worst pressure of the evening. We kept fairly well to time, but now and then it was held up a little. Of course we talked in the composing room as we worked, but we were as quick as we could be, and in the end, instead of just standing and watching, I sometimes hurried things by handling galleys of type against all trade-union rules.

Mr R. stormed one night when the page was a few minutes late. Wag bowed to his wrath and, as far as I could gather, agreed that we could do better and any lateness was my fault. Mr R. strode into my room and forbade me to go up to the composing room again. In his suspicion of women he no doubt believed that I was wasting the men's time, playing about up there, holding up the paper. And Wag, in the subservience that I noticed in the men, said not a word in my defence; rather put the blame on me.

The next few evenings were chaotic. All the cutting and arranging had to be done from my room, which was a long way from the composing room. Wag, bent on satisfying the imperial will, ran up and down and shouted. Printers and readers came to and fro, and by concentration on the one page and a skimping of corrections we managed to be finished before ten.

Then the fuss subsided. It was quite impossible to make up the page in that way, and Mr R., having put the fear of the Lord into us, turned to something else. When I began to go up to the composing room again, nothing was said.

And nothing very terrible happened generally in the office. Gradually Mr R. settled down. He was a great talker and would come in and tell stories of Lady That or old Sir George X, and I would smile dutifully. He also had friends whom he invited to write for the women's page, and so perhaps grew more reconciled to women's intrusion in newspaper production.

Some of the men staff went to visit him. He had taken an expensive flat, and they reported that he had 'some lovely things'. But, in spite of his aristocratic friends, he may well have been lonely.

He was kind to me in the end. When the war came and I offered to resign he would not let me, and, when finally I did leave, he arranged for me to have a retaining fee and write articles for the paper.

Towards the end of the war he became unwell. He said it was indigestion caused by wartime bread, but it turned out to be cancer. Finally he was moved to hospital, and I heard that office people had been to see him and reported that he was still 'talking nineteen to the dozen' and not letting them get a word in. But he died quite soon, and Mr L.P.H. who had been passed over before, at last became editor, though for only a short time.

Editors, I have found, are not a very estimable race. Plato would say they have too much authority. Mr R. was by no means the worst that I have known.

Events

One Saturday midday, when I was going home for the weekend, I saw on New Street Station a poster saying 'Insurrection in Spain'. I breathed a sigh of relief. 'Nothing very serious comes out of Spain,' I thought. It is perhaps lucky that we cannot see the future.

Though the 'thirties seem now a long anticipation of war, there were many other events to occupy us at the time. General elections always provided an evening of excitement at the Daily. The editorial staff would get its work done early to leave time and space for the results, and we would stand at the long windows of the editor's room that looked across New Street. An arrangement would have been made to shine the results, as they came in, on to a sheet on a building opposite, and a small crowd would collect below to watch. Our room would be in half darkness with the lights turned off, and we would be, as it were, in a theatre box with the best view. It was exciting, though with my vaguely left-wing views I would be irritated when the Daily's bosses and one or two parliamentary candidates came in flushed and triumphant.

They would have had drinks in the manager's room next door and would be in animated joyful conversation. The candidate I chiefly remember was Geoffrey Lloyd, Unionist member for Ladywood, tall, handsome and young. The Conservatives were coming to power, and our bosses were pleased that so many well-known local figures would be in the government, including the Chamberlains with their long past, Stanley Baldwin, son of a Worcestershire iron master, and Anthony Eden, the rising star who was cousin to the Earl of Warwick.

Meanwhile the royal family was giving us plenty to talk about. First the old King was ill; then he recovered, celebrated his jubilee on the throne, and then died. Edward VIII who had been 'Prince Charming', became a figure of dark rumours. Mrs Simpson began to appear in newspaper pictures. Our own Midland Baldwin was behind the abdication, and the Daily wrote solemn leaders approving. Birmingham, with Worcestershire porcelain and Staffordshire pottery firms, had busily prepared souvenirs for one coronation and then had to scrap them, but more coronation souvenirs were required in 1937. All the royal crises caused long waits and extra work at newspaper offices, for announcements were often thoughtlessly late at night.

Of course, other home issues turned our eyes inwards. In the early 'thirties it was unemployment and the hunger marches; later the burning question of rearmament, though that naturally was linked with Hitler. Campaigns were going on all the time, though not for a 'green' world or with trailing processions and banners. In Birmingham some of us were much concerned with the horror of capital punishment, and we read books such as the ironic *Handbook of Hanging* by Charles Duff, took in penal reform literature and sent contributions to anti-capital punishment societies. The newspaper stories of the last moments of a condemned man, photographs of protesters waiting in the early morning outside prisons, and a warder coming out at just after eight to pin up a notice that the execution had taken place, made our hearts miss a beat. The climax of the horror was to be the Nuremberg hangings after the war, to be followed by the enormous feeling of relief when capital punishment was abolished in Britain.

There were other causes, many focusing on Christian works including missions to darkest Africa. But international threats crept on us gradually. British men were killed in the Spanish civil war. German refugees were becoming noticeable in England. ''Oo is this 'ere Ilter?' one old Summer Lane lady asked me in about 1937.

But all this time we continued to go abroad for holidays and return to comment on the friendliness of the peoples of Europe. We said happily that the exchange was in our favour, that holidays abroad were as cheap as British ones, not thinking that these financial benefits might not be popular with our host countries. My first fortnight in Italy, with railway fares and hotel bills, cost £15. With that kind of expenditure we could go blithely to France and Spain and then finally – without bothering about Hitler – to Germany.

One summer we did not know that we should be taking part in history, and hardly had any feeling of adventure. I was only mildly surprised when the Thomas Cook office in Birmingham said it could not book us hotel rooms in Nuremberg because for the days when we wanted them they would be full up with Germans themselves

attending Hitler's Parteitag. You could always get something when
you were on the spot, I thought, and we had decided on a trip to
Vienna, travelling by stages up the Rhine and taking a Danube boat
at Linz.

So began the excursion which at first half turned us into Nazis.
Everything went well till we were in the German train heading south.
As usual on continental long-distance trains, conversations began,
and the English Fräuleins were asked where they were going. When
we said Nuremberg, smiles of surprise went round. Had we rooms?
No. Well . . . Did we know about the Parteitag? We had just heard of
it but did that matter?

'Never mind,' two polite German men said. 'We will try to help
you.'

When we alighted on the Nuremberg platform they conducted us
to some bureau and introduced us as two young English ladies who
were so anxious to see Hitler that we had come without having been
able to book rooms. Not only were all the hotels full but private
families were opening their homes to visitors, all for the love of the
Führer. We might have been forced to sleep on the station but it
happened that one visitor had had to go home through illness, and
there was just one room vacant. It was allotted to us because of our
interest in Nazism.

Feeling deceivers but not quite sure of our disapproval because of
all the obvious joy around us, we were introduced to the Göss family,
simple people who then devoted themselves to showing us the city
and fostering our love of Hitler. The streets were hung with garlands,
banners and symbols. People leaned out of windows calling greetings
and everybody was transformed with joy.

We were a little comatose through spending the previous night in
travel, and we began to wonder if perhaps Britain should have been
more sympathetic to the Nazis. The family took us to a Bierkeller
where people were drinking and laughing, and after dark to a fair in
Hitler's honour, with oxen being roasted whole and milling crowds.
A group of soldiers followed us laughing and shouting, 'Dicker-
dacker, dicker-dacker, hoy hoy hoy' (English spelling) and may have
been mocking the English visitors. Warlike toys were on sale
everywhere, and the Gösses' little son Karl, aged seven, had a
complete Nazi uniform.

But the next morning, when we were clearer headed, doubts began
to rise. In the street we saw two poor little figures creeping along by
a wall, and our hosts nudged us and said 'Jews' with intense scorn.

Outside a church was a board of regulations with such ferocious orders against Jews that we were appalled.

Our family wanted us to wait and see Hitler, who was due to parade the streets, but we were not enough bemused as to change our itinerary. We went along to the station through streets thronged with onlookers, with boys climbing the lampposts to see better. I had asked the Gösses what was the best German paper I could buy, and they had recommended *Der Stürmer*, 'a very good paper'. It turned out to be the ill-famed Jew-baiting organ, and one glance disgusted us. We did not buy it.

After Nuremberg the journey seemed very quiet and we felt as if we were emerging from a dream. Later, when we carelessly said in a boat on the Danube that we had been at the Parteitag at Nuremberg, there was a sudden stony silence. Then somebody said coldly that in Austria they knew nothing of what the Germans were doing, and we had a feeling of the tension Hitler was causing. This was, of course, before the Anschluss when Hitler marched into Vienna.

For conscience's sake we did not return to Nuremberg though the Gösses invited us. But Frau Göss was a faithful correspondent, and we exchanged letters till the war. After the war we sent food parcels to the old address. The father was dead, and the small Karl had been in the army – at the age of about fourteen. Frau Göss wrote, 'We did not want war.'

Even as war threatened I was still anxious to hear German spoken, but I did not want to spend money in Hitler's Reich. One year we temporised and had a holiday in Holland, crossing the German border for only a few days. But even then we came up against the Nazis, for in a Cologne street we met one of Hitler's groups marching. All the crowds raised arms in a Hitler salute, but we would not honour him and stood with our arms rigidly by our sides. We expected to be arrested, but nobody took any notice of us.

Through the 'thirties a new charity appeared, particularly fostered by the Quakers. Governments were abominably slow in receiving Jewish refugees, and one Berlin teacher told us afterwards how queues went from embassy to embassy begging admission to some country outside Germany. She and her sister gained admittance only because as a reader of *The Times* she saw notices about the Home Office, and thought it was a department that provided homes. So she wrote directly to it, and her letter was passed to the Quakers.

At the end of the period you could pay so much – a little less than £100, I think – to get a Jew out of Germany. Most refugees hoped for the United States as an ultimate home, but they began the journey in Britain. The scheme was functioning when war was declared, but thousands were left to death at the concentration camps. It was most difficult when a person was handicapped, as nobody wanted him. I was negotiating for the escape of a hump-backed young man, a relative of a family already in England, when war came, and he too went to a concentration camp and died there.

As the threat from Germany became more apparent Birmingham people used to ask me for news. They thought that, because I worked on a paper, I should know more than the general public. Actually, of course, I knew only the news that came in, though I knew it a bit earlier than outside people. When Hitler was going to make what was prophesied would be an important evening speech, I would ask Wag to come down about midnight and give me news of it. He was always good at news-mongering, and he would appear cheerfully and say, ''Ere, vere was nothing in it.' For there generally was nothing solid in Hitler's speeches. It was his actions that caused the war.

We must have been very apprehensive in 1938, for we decided to go to Ireland to avoid Europe. At Killarney we were far away, both physically and mentally, from the excitement of the Munich meetings. We did call at a small shop for papers, always late, but we had a feeling of freedom, as if the European situation did not matter much in a world of leprechauns and jaunting cars. Later in Birmingham I found, when I got back, that anxiety was tempered by pride in Neville Chamberlain, the son of the city, who, though an old man unable to speak German, had had the courage to make long journeys for personal discussions with Hitler. He was to have a bad press later, but more justice has been done to him since.

In the 'thirties we used to argue what we should do if war broke out. We declared that it was better to be killed than kill and an invasion of Britain better than war. The memory of 1914-18 was still strong, and most of the young people at any rate were pacifists at heart. But when the event finally occurred private people were not asked. Hitler invaded Poland, and one government came in after another.

There was one apparently poetical utterance that I treasured in those days. It was: 'We must follow the light as we see the light,' and it came from the king, George VI, when he made a patriotic broadcast. For me it linked with the Bible utterance of the light shining in darkness. It was only later that I learned that the king, with his speech impediment, had said, 'We must follow the right as we see the right' – a noble sentiment but not as poetic.

War

The situation in the summer of 1939 was so threatening that we wondered if we should have a holiday abroad. But one thing the war was to show was that people continued their normal occupations as far as possible even while the world was falling apart round them; and we were like the rest. For years we had had holidays in Europe; we wanted to see the Katherine Mansfield country in the south of France – and we argued that it was unlikely that war would break out exactly in the fortnight while we were away.

Tourists are detached, of course, from the ordinary life of a country, and though I read some French papers there seemed not much more flurry about Hitler than usual. Then one sunny hot morning we walked down the main street of Cézanne's Arles and became aware of groups talking in low voices in cafés. They were earnest and quiet, and I imagined that some local disaster had taken place. In the end we asked. The man, as far as I remember, was unwilling to say much but muttered something about 'la guerre'. We bought a paper then and read that call-up notices were expected to go up on the *mairies*.

What to do? We had come a long way and had been in France for only a few days. There were no other English people about. It seemed easy to stay on and enjoy the sun. We were used to alarms anyway. On the other hand we might be stranded. We decided to temporise; to move to Marseilles which had quick trains to Paris.

When we reached Marseilles in the late afternoon there was no doubt as to what we should do. The call-up was official, and French holidaying families as well as foreign tourists were hurrying home. The train service was in chaos, but we were told that an express for Paris was due, and presently, with a great seething multitude on the platform, it steamed in. Then there was a rush, with people struggling and pushing up the high steps. We were in at last, and I have not forgotten the feeling of relief.

But it was a terrifying night. All the French stations were blacked out so that we had no idea where we were. A thunderstorm raged, and the flashes seemed somehow connected with the war. The train was jammed with anxious French people, and we sat on our bags in the corridor. As the sky at last paled with dawn the tension slackened a little. We were in the environs of Paris and, as the train stopped at a small station, several men leapt out to buy newspapers. They brought them back. 'Pas encore.' War had not yet been declared.

The train rolled into the terminus, and the hordes hurried away. In the chill of seven o'clock, Paris seemed itself, men dusting tables outside cafés and girls tripping to work. Was all the fuss about nothing? But when we reached the Gare St Lazare the feeling of panic returned. Again there were the seething crowds. Holiday-makers were returning from all over Europe and North Africa. Excited English voices mixed with the buzz of conversation, and tourists exchanged confidences on their journeys. Now there was an urgent pushing into the Dieppe train, and when it stopped at the port people scrambled out and waited in a close crowd. I thought, 'Suppose a German bomber comes now . . .'

But no bomber came, and when we reached England it seemed dull and unchanged, with its lines of suburban houses and grey Victoria terminus. The papers had large headlines, but nothing definite had yet happened. We went to our Surrey home to sleep.

A day or two of doubt remained. I remember passing a *Daily Express* poster in Fleet Street. 'There will be no war,' it proclaimed, and if offered prizes to readers if it should be wrong. Louis from Stuttgart, a refugee staying at my home, asserted that if we would only stand up to the 'raffinierte Hunde' in Germany they would draw back.

International panics do not entirely swamp self-interest. One happy memory accompanies those tense days. For the Daily's London Letter editor wrote to ask if I were back – a sign that I was still wanted – and also asked if I would write something of my experiences in France. Now all through the years I had been confined to 'Women's Interests', always the 'little woman', excluded from the editorial meetings and the great male stream of things. It seemed almost beyond belief that these important London men wanted something of me.

Joyfully I wrote two paragraphs on France and they were published. Later ones, quoting Louis's call to stand up to Hitler, were not.

Outbreak

There must still be many people who remember the way the conflict began on a Sunday morning, when the sad radio voice of Neville Chamberlain told us that we were at war with Germany. Nobody had the slightest idea of what to expect, and when the sirens went by mistake, somebody thinking that German planes were crossing the Channel, we were sure that we should be gassed and raced down to our semi-basement kitchen and put wet towels over our faces. Outside, the garden remained sunny and peaceful, and soon the all-clear sounded and we thought it might be safe to emerge – for a short distance anyway.

The coming of war made people do strange things. One was to destroy their pets. Throughout the country vets' surgeries were besieged by people applying for euthanasia for their dogs and cats. Presumably they were afraid that their animals might suffer in the coming catastrophe, but the wave of animal destruction was beyond reason – an epidemic. Many pet-owners must have been sorry later.

My reaction was also beyond reason. I returned to Birmingham and told Mr R. that I expected that he would want me to leave.

But already war was making us all more kindly. To my surprise Mr R. said I was not to go. The Daily would no doubt be rationed for paper, and 'Women's Interests' would have to stop, but I would still be wanted. He remembered from the First World War how men had been called up and women had been needed to take their place. 'Don't think of leaving. We shall need you.'

Then I knew that I should have hated to go. Birmingham had become my home. I did not want to leave any of them.

What work was I to do? 'Well,' said Mr R., 'I want to keep some local interest going. Otherwise we shall become just a copy of the London papers. Suppose you write articles on what local organisations are doing in the war?'

Delightful suggestion. I was to be kept. I could go where I liked, write what I liked. And of course the war would be over in a few months, and we would return to the old life.

All the same it was sad to stop the old evening activities; no longer to go into Ned's room to look through photographs; no longer to go up to the composing room to make up a page; no longer to open many long envelopes with articles; to tell the writers of the few that did arrive that we could take no more 'for the duration'. I should have felt it more if I had not, like everybody else, been overwhelmed with the sense of change. Some Germans, even intellectuals, thought that war elevated the soul of a nation. Certainly people were kinder than usual and ready for sacrifice. A librarian told me that much more poetry was being taken out by the public. Later, of course, the public mind was to become callous and dulled to horrors, and people – as I was to find to my cost – would go round making idiotic statements such as 'the only good German is a dead 'un'.

And yet in many ways the world had not changed interest in fashion for example. We were all issued with gas masks in black metal holders and told not to go out without them. The holders were adequate to contain the beastly masks and could be hung on the arm. But immediately shops began to sell more elegant gas-mask containers, and many people – women at any rate – bought them. Another favourite purchase was bracelets with name tags so that if we were killed in an air raid we should be identifiable. Then there was all the talk about the kind of material one should use for the blackout. It was an opportunity to buy special stuff.

Also, as in a stirred up hive, people became hyperactive. New organisations were set up – the Women's Voluntary Services, the Citizens' Advice Bureaux. But I felt as usual a little apart from the main stream of behaviour, and went poking into odd corners of Birmingham.

Flower Girls and Horses

In those first autumn days I spent the afternoons trailing round to charities and societies, and went back to the office in the evening. There was plenty still to be done in the evening – arrangement for visits to be made, articles to be written, proofs to be read, letters to be sent, for people were still submitting their own articles. However in the early months of the war I left earlier, for I was told by Mr R. to be out of the office by ten. He did not want women on his hands in air raids. He was not to know what was coming.

He had asked for articles on the effects of war, and, afraid of not being useful, I did one nearly every day. I could write about the flurry of new activities and the hospitals, which were sending normal patients home in dozens to have beds ready for air-raid casualties. As no raids occurred in the early months, they increased their numbers of patients again. I had to find other topics, but there is always something you can write about a hospital, as television has shown.

But then, as we settled down for the winter and grew used to the blackout and rationing, I could not go on writing about war activities only. With all these articles I had to find an enormous number of subjects. Birmingham was full of charities and voluntary enterprises which had been only superficially affected by the war, but the war theme made an excuse for a visit, and their histories were often entertaining. I was soon absorbed in Birmingham history. Ancient minute books, not studied since Victorian days, were brought out from dusty cupboards. They recorded in their ugly spiky writing the rules of children's homes or the opening of parks, and they showed many earnest and sometimes self-important people exercising their talents in small fields.

Almost invariably the organisations were glad of publicity. I was given cups of tea, though tea was rationed, and I remember a blazing fire and a plate of potato scones in a hospital matron's room. 'Our cook is good at potato scones.' I had letters of thanks afterwards. It was all very pleasant – except that the war was still on.

But when you have been writing on institutions for months, your subjects, even in a town as large as Birmingham, begin to grow thin. I used to rack my brains on where I could go next. I was interested in people as well as organisations, and one friend suggested an interview with a woman looking after public lavatories, but I never risked that.

But I did try the Corporation Street flower-sellers. There they stood with their kerb-side baskets making splashes of colour among the ugly buildings and traffic, and I had sometimes bought a bunch of snowdrops or violets or the wild daffodils they brought in from Gloucestershire fields. When you were a customer they called you 'lady' and held out their bunches and were very oily in their manners. I was used to talking to humble people, and I thought they might tell me something about their job and lives.

So one afternoon I went up to one, and she thought I was a customer and put on a welcoming smile. But she did not look as pleased when I told her that I was writing about Birmingham people and wanted her to help me.

She was half-suspicious, half-yielding, when a flower seller beside her shouted, 'Don't you tell her nothing. Don't you talk to her.'

Passers-by were beginning to eye us, but I waited. My lady then informed me that she made no money, absolutely nothing, by her flower-selling – if anything lost money. When I asked her why she sold flowers then, she turned her back and began to offer flowers to other pedestrians. I lingered a moment, but it was hopeless. The other girls stood dumbly with sour stony faces. The article on flower girls' finances never got written.

But I was a little luckier with the paper-sellers. For years I had heard stories of them from Bert, the cheerful young man in the back office. He had told me that they were a wild lot, often drunk, sometimes in prison; and they had their own rhyming slang – 'tit-for-tat' for hat, 'cup of tea' for three. One of them, a gigantic fellow, was nicknamed Titch.

They sold evening papers at street corners, each with his own beat. Their shouts of 'Spetch-i-My' ('Despatch and Mail') would rise above the noise of traffic in the afternoon in the centre of town. When the bundles of paper were being issued from our side entrance the sellers would be a menace, rushing in, seizing their bundles and charging down the sloping narrow street like madmen, intent on getting first on to the streets. Several times they had nearly knocked me over.

Bert suggested that I should come in when the bundles were being distributed, stand and watch by the rough wooden counter and try to converse with some of them. He alerted the man who handed out the papers that I would be there, but told me to be wary, as the sellers had short tempers.

It was a winter afternoon, and the sellers charged in with caps and mufflers. They looked at me suspiciously, flung down rattling coins, seized their bundles with hardly a word and rushed out. It was not easy to interview them as, like the flower girls, they were suspicious and they wanted to get to their street corners.

But one elderly man was persuaded to make a few remarks. He had his beat by the central Post Office, one of the town's landmarks with its French château style. His father had sold papers there before him, and he regarded the corner as family property. He seemed – at least in talking to me – to take a serious view of his job, saying that he tried to oblige his customers and people knew him. He had been selling papers there for forty years.

His finances were unintelligible. He paid a shilling for each bundle of thirteen papers and sold each paper for a penny. So he made a profit of just one penny on each bundle. I felt that he could not be giving me a full account of his earnings, and I asked Bert about paper-sellers' finances afterwards. He said that the sellers probably offered other services as well – took bets.

Of course an obvious subject for articles would have been the canals which were beginning to carry more goods in the wartime emergency. But, strange as it seems today, Birmingham was in the 'thirties little aware of its waterways. The railways had taken over transport the century before, and the canals were foul and neglected, visible only as an occasional dark gleam between dirty fences in back streets. When I first went to Birmingham I knew nothing about canals and for years was ignorant of them. They were mostly seen in the country, often running in a peculiar way along the tops of hills, with brick bridges over low lanes. They were mainly used by fishermen, who came out at weekends and left an ungodly mess of rubbish, uncollected, along their banks.

I should have been amazed if I had been told that canal restoration was to be pursued so fervently after the war, and that the Birmingham network was to become a tourist attraction. Now it was some time before I thought of writing of canals, but it seemed after weeks that the boat people might have something to say. On a gloomy autumn afternoon I followed directions and turned off from Broad Street along a narrow shabby street that I had hardly noticed before.

Presently I came to a high wall, and behind the wall was a stretch of water. A signpost marked the canals that came in from different areas – London, the north, the west. In the windy gloom, with dark rippling water, one or two boats were tied up, with their traditional decorations of roses and castles. A group of canal people was standing by the boats – weather-beaten faces old before their time with shabby thick clothes. When I began to talk to them I met the same suspicion as I had met in the flower girls. They were afraid of being exploited, and their half answers were very different from the glib harangues given by workers today on television.

I tried the subject of children. Welfare workers had told me of the difficulties of their education as, in the way of the gipsies, most of their lives was spent travelling. There was now a school for canal children in Birmingham as well as in London, but they attended only while boats were being unloaded. This meant that they were a group apart, with little prospect of breaking away from narrow-boat life and little contact with the rest of the world.

The boat people were certainly suspicious when I tried to ask questions. Aye, the children were now at school. Aye, times were a bit better than they had been. Not that they made much money. Not they! Yes, they had been on the waterways all their lives. Well, it wasn't bad. You didn't feel the cold much.

It was a small harvest, but I managed to write something, together with canal history and official facts about the war situation. However that afternoon, having spent only a short time with one group of survivors from the past, I went on to another. Near the canal basin was one of the stables for Birmingham Corporation horses. The corporation had said that I could go and look at the horses and had given me the addresses of the stables. Horses were still about the streets in the 'thirties, mainly used for heavy loads. The Summer Lane people still talked of the 'horse road', and with the war, horse traffic had been increased.

I found the stables – low brick buildings with cobbles, wafting around the country smell of hay and dung. On that afternoon there was only one great horse in its stall. The rest were out working. But one or two stable hands were about, and here at last were people willing to talk.

Both sexes of horses, I was told, were used to pull heavy loads. You could not say that males were better than females. Some were bad-tempered; some placid. They were like human beings. They all had different temperaments. And in another way they were like men and women. They were given a rest on Sundays, and Monday was their black day. They were unwilling to work, but then got into routine again and improved as the week went on.

The stable hands were obviously fond of their charges, and their stories made a change from all the factories I visited with their lines of automated and unintelligible machines. At first I had not thought of going to factories as they were targets for bombs, but I found that my visits were welcomed as long as I did not give their addresses. There was plenty to say about them apart from details of war production – their history, their workpeople, their welfare arrangements.

It was the newer firms that were introducing 'music while you work' and canteens. Other visits were like a return to the early Industrial Revolution. One I made was to a foundry in the Black Country, and I visited it on a cold winter day. I found the works like a great open barn with furnaces dotted about. Periodically one or other furnace door would be opened, and out would pour a stream of sparking, hissing, molten metal. It ran into long channels and changed from a pale glare to a red glow and finally blackness.

The building was freezingly cold in the spaces but blindingly hot in front of the open furnaces. The men, who seemed mainly old and gnarled, looked like devils of hell against the glare. The long working day must have been acutely uncomfortable and exhausting as well as monotonous, but they seemed a cheerful lot, proudly boasting in their strong Black Country accents of how long they had been on the job.

It was my industrial visits that were to lead to my parting from the Daily.

Bombs

During the air raids you could never tell exactly what was happening elsewhere. The newspapers veered between sob stories and minimising the damage and, at the beginning at any rate, one always thought that one was suffering more than other people. After Birmingham's first raid I wrote home saying that I was not dead. My family was surprised. They did not know that Birmingham had had any bombs.

Birmingham's first casualty was a school – empty because the raid had been at night in the weekend. The next day crowds assembled to stare at the broken roof and windows. Their attitude, I think, was awe and pride. This terrible thing was actually happening to their city. By chance I was being driven along the main road. 'Look – there,' the driver said, but we passed too quickly for me to see much. There were just all those people gazing up and talking.

Mr R.'s command that I should leave the office at ten amused the printers, since he was known to dislike women. 'Thinks you'd be a liability,' they said. He had not apparently considered that I might be caught by a raid on the way home.

It should have been easy enough to leave by ten, but it was not. I was generally out gathering material in the afternoon so that I did not come into the office early. Now I seemed always to be watching the clock. As usual at about 8.30 a canteen lady would come down with the bountiful tray, which still included a glass of cold milk. I used to leave this and then gulp it hurriedly before I left. It was terribly indigestible and lay like lead within.

The office was warm, bright and cheerful behind its blackout. I had to step out into the utter dark void of the side alley. At first one could see nothing. Then I had to hurry along New Street to the

Town Hall to catch the last bus that would take me home. I was always afraid that I should miss it or that the siren would go before I got in. I ran along the middle of the road to avoid stumbling over the Fire Service pipes now out along the kerbs. Often I would be chewing a bun that I had not had time to eat before. It did not matter. Nobody could see me.

But soon the raids began earlier. Sometimes the siren's wail curdled the blood even before one reached the office. I remember the wail suddenly swelling as I was crossing the churchyard after an afternoon in Summer Lane. I ran to the office as to a haven. It gave one a roof over one's head and companions.

Presently raids became so much part of the early evening that one could not settle down to work until the sirens sounded. The previous silence seemed ominous – everyone holding his breath. When at last we heard the wail we seized our papers and typewriters, turned off our fires and lights and started on a long downward trek. Round passages and through doors we walked in that warren of a building till we came to an obscure flight of stairs. Down and down past huge machines the procession went till it reached a depth two storeys below ground level. Here were the great presses that printed the paper, humming and shaking the ground when they were at work but silent at that time in the evening.

As we descended the air grew warmer and our sense of security greater. As usual class distinctions were observed. The printers had their own room and we had ours – from Mr R. to the sub-editors. Here we settled to work, but the printers went up and down in quiet moments, for they had to return to the composing room to get on with the paper. The raids brought out the best in everybody, and the printers, led by Wag, worked away upstairs till the 'imminent danger' signal went.

I never discovered how far the honeycomb of chambers, with their whitewashed walls, extended, but they went right under the street to an office on the other side. We were told to run if we were going from one side to the other, as the connecting passage was only one storey below ground level. The readers would wander to and fro bringing proofs. As the raids became routine people grew more venturous, and Wag drew me up to the composing room to get my articles fitted in. We seemed to be going right up to the heavens, by stairs after stairs to the top of the building. The composing room had a glass roof shielded, of course, but vulnerable, and aircraft always seemed to be droning about overhead. I was a coward and hurried to get through, but the men worked with concentration, and presently Wag and some of them would go on with their jobs even when the imminent danger signal had sounded.

Early in the raids Birmingham's most elegant dress shop, Warwick House, facing our office across Corporation Street, was burned down. At the time preparations for air raids were casual, and there was no compulsory fire-watching. The old caretaker had locked up and gone home when a shower of firebombs fell on the city. There was nobody to detect the Warwick House blaze till it was fully flaring. Then the police came, but they could not get in. Nor did anybody know where the caretaker lived. Soon a tremendous conflagration soared over the blacked-out city. It was a mercy, people said afterwards, that the Germans did not take more advantage of it and come back with large bombs.

''Ere,' Wag said to me. 'Come and 'ave a look.' He drew me, rather unwilling, to a composing room window with a view of Corporation Street. Flames were leaping from an inferno opposite and flaring across the street, which in the haze appeared quite narrow. It seemed as if we too would catch fire at any moment. Somebody brought a message that we must prepare to leave in a hurry. But by now the Fire Service had arrived and the hoses were playing, and, though they could not save Warwick House, they prevented us from catching alight. Presently the blaze sank a little and then turned to a glow. The next day when I came in to work I found Birmingham's most elegant store, with its furs, dresses and perfumes, a black charred mass at ground level, wafting out that acrid smell of burning that was to become so familiar.

When we were down below we seemed cut off from the world, but the men had discovered one way of seeing out. An immense chimney shaft, relic of another age, went up from the vaults to the sky. You could stand underneath it and look what seemed miles up and see the stars. Sometimes, when fires were burning, the clouds were tinged with red, and on the night of Coventry's great raid an expanse of sky was bright pink. A man coming down from fire-watching on the roof reported that 'people were getting it hot over there', and soon we knew by telephone that the target was Coventry.

Birmingham afterwards was a little jealous of Coventry's fame as a martyr. 'Just as much has fallen on us,' people said. 'But we're bigger, and the damage doesn't show as much.' Noticeable in the raids was this rivalry of suffering. Each area thought it was the worst.

The provincial towns were jealous of London's bombing fame, and they were jealous of one another.

There were plenty of incidents in those winter months, and always the Daily men – the lower ranks, not the elderly editorial group – behaved admirably. 'Coo,' said one man, looking up from the street when the raid was over, 'however did I do it?' He had been climbing about the roofs all night knocking firebombs off the building. He had brought down a jagged heavy piece of metal – a piece of shell from our own guns. We were frequently urged to remember that 'what goes up has to come down'.

I was upstairs in the composing room one night when the remains of a firebomb was brought down and passed from hand to hand. It was an ugly tarnished metal frame, rather in the shape of a large pepper pot and still almost too hot to hold. Along its rim was an assembly of figures and letters. We wished we knew what they meant.

Once, as we sat down below, somebody came in and whispered a message into the ear of George, the sub-editor who was so kind to me and so merry generally. His face stiffened and he got up and disappeared. Then the news came that he had been wanted on the telephone. His wife and young daughter had been sitting in an air-raid shelter at the end of their garden, and it had been hit. They were both hurt and in hospital, and the neighbour with them had been killed. By an irony of fate their house, from which they had taken refuge, was untouched. They did, however, recover.

One evening the word went round, 'Teddy's arrived. He says the station has gone.' Teddy was the friendly printer whom I called Pimmy. Later he came into our rooms to report, his light brown hair ruffled, his face grey and sunken as George's had been. 'There'll never be a New Street Station again,' he said.

It had been his late shift, but he had apparently never thought of not coming in to work from his distant suburb of Yardley. Since buses were uncertain, being taken off the road in raids, he had started on his bicycle. Near the centre of Birmingham 'so much stuff was dropping' that he had put the bicycle over the hedge of an unknown garden and continued on foot. Just as he arrived at the station, which he had to cross to reach the office, it received a direct hit. He skirted round it somehow and at last reached the office, but the experience had made him look an old man. Actually, as so often happened, the damage was not as bad as it had seemed at first, and in a few days part of the station was working again.

Then there came the night when the office itself got a direct hit.

We could hear the bombs approaching – first a distant boom, then louder, then louder still and then an almighty crash. All the lights went out, and a trickle of dust and plaster flaked down on our heads. When I came to myself, I found I had jumped right away from the wall by which I had been sitting. Immediately voices began in the darkness. 'All right? Are you all right?' and almost at once somebody brought in candles. We endured in the flickering light for that night, but the next evening the electricity was on again. But the bomb had caused severe damage, for it had hit some heavy machinery and sent it crashing down to the floor below.

Sometimes stranded people, including women whom Mr R. had wanted out of the building, found their way to our vaults. Generally, as dusk fell, the streets cleared like magic, but these people had lingered too long. Once the lady who touched up the photographs appeared with two strangers. She said she had been waiting at the bus stop and there had been a rattle like a stick running along railings, and everywhere round them seemed to burst into flame. She ran for the office, bringing the stranded people with her. They joined us for cups of tea but had to wait for most of the night, for the raids were now going on for hours.

Some of the nights seemed interminable. The longest raid continued for nearly twelve hours. The printers finished their work on the now thin newspaper, and the vans rushed across country to some station that still had a train running to London. Then the printers waited, dozing, eating sandwiches and playing darts. Round about dawn the shelters became both stuffy and chilly.

Through the long nights messages usually came in from the London staff who were also working from cellars. But once or twice communication ceased because the telephone lines were down between London and Birmingham. Still somehow the paper was brought out. Once the rival paper 'up the street' offered to let us share its facilities. It was a time when everybody was kinder than usual.

Presently we began to start for home before the all-clear went. Once in a lull I went to my room to get my things and switched on my light. It was only after a few minutes that I realised that my high window with its blackout had fallen open with the impact of bombs nearby, and my light was streaming straight up to heaven. I expected a rain of bombs, but the raiders must have been somewhere else.

It was an intimidating moment when we came out into the night with a raid still on. Everything was dead black, and planes were still droning away far overhead. Once we emerged with our street glistening in the moonlight. The windows round had been shattered, and glass fragments were all over the place. 'Keep in the middle of the road,' we were told, 'and you'll be less likely to get your shoes cut' The coaches were waiting in New Street at the bottom of the alley to avoid cut tyres.

The coaches came for us whenever they could get through, but it was a problem to reach home. Nobody knew what had happened to the streets. Sometimes to drive westward we had first to go southeast as all the other roads were blocked. But we circled past barriers and ruins till we turned in the right direction at last. We had to skirt fallen bricks, and once I saw from the bus a glaring window where people seemed to have forgotten to put up the blackout. 'Somebody should tell them,' I thought, and then I realised that the roof of the house had been blown off, and the dawn sky was shining through the socket of a window.

Once or twice, however, our coaches could not reach us and we had to walk home. Once I came out when a fierce fire was burning near. I heard what I thought was the throb-throb of bombing aircraft overhead and turned to go back to the office. Then I realised that the throbbing was coming from the pumps fighting the fire, and I walked on.

I came to the churchyard in the centre of Birmingham. A full moon, very small, white and distant, was up behind the bare branches of a plane tree. It looked incongruous above the red light of the fires; yet serene and a relic of a past world.

Presently a man from the office joined me, and we walked on together. We passed the Town Hall and reached Broad Street; and there we met a crowd watching a burning building that was about to collapse. Among the people was a man with a bandaged head. He must have been hit somehow. It was tempting to wait and see the flaming walls crash down, but we had a long way to walk and we wanted our beds. 'Hurry,' a fireman said as we sidled past the building, and so we tramped on and left the sightseers. After that the Edgbaston suburbs seemed very quiet and peaceful.

Yet in the weekends when I was not at the office I felt threatened more than when I was with all those protective brave men. In our flats at the corner of the street we now had a table shelter with its thick shiny metal slab under which one climbed when danger was near. The tables had been issued when the Anderson shelters in the gardens had proved impossible to use in winter. Our table shelter blocked our downstairs hall, but when the guns were going I came down and joined the two ground-floor ladies. In the early raids, when no-one knew what was going to happen, they brought large saucepans and at dangerous moments put them on their heads. They might have been a protection if a bomb had fallen on us, but it did not fall.

We were nervous as we sat there with our table. One of the effects of blackout and sirens was to make one feel isolated and ignorant of what was happening outside. 'Was that a bomb?' said one jumpy lady.

'No. It was only my tummy rumbling,' said the other.

Later the ladies arranged to shelter in the cellar of acquaintances further down the street, and I was invited to go at weekends. I remember walking quite calmly in my nightdress along the road and meeting a soldier who as calmly bade me goodnight. All kinds of conventions were disappearing at the time, including that of wearing a hat.

But the cellar nights were uncomfortable. We were cramped, and we had as companion the family's parrot which screamed now and then. As soon as the all-clear sounded we rose stiffly and trailed back to our beds.

And there was our house on the corner standing as solid as ever. The only damage we ever found was a trickle of plaster and dust fallen from the ceiling of the porch – dislodged when a bomb fell near. So we might have stayed in our beds all the time.

In the raids we all had our chosen havens, and felt unsafe when we were anywhere else. At dusk when bombing was worst one could see family groups with their bedding setting out for their chosen shelters.

Once, when I had come home for the weekend and was walking up from our Surrey station, the sirens went. In this different territory I did not know what to do. How likely were bombs to fall on this area of polite houses and gardens?

I passed a surface shelter and went in. A man from the street did the same. We stood rather foolishly waiting for something to happen, but nothing did. After a few minutes the man got tired of waiting and walked out. Then I did the same, and still nothing happened.

Towards the end of the war, when Birmingham was safe, the London area was suffering from flying and rocket bombs. They were without targets and might fall anywhere, and when you heard them you did not know where they had come down. One night at home I was awakened by two enormous crashes, but one could do nothing about them so turned over and went to sleep again.

I recently discovered a letter written on 21 October 1940 to my sister.

I am writing from the Post having just got back from Chedworth [Gloucestershire, where I had been having a weekend break]. A good thing I didn't try London. Trains from New St seem completely suspended, and I met a woman from Streatham, evacuating her old mother, on the way down; and she said Paddington was a seething mass and she missed her first train because she had to wait 1¼ hours for a ticket. My own train to Cheltenham was 2½ hours late. There have been bombs here on the railways, and trains are apparently going by all sorts of side lines.

I hope nothing too awful has happened at Surbiton. We have had a lively week. A bomb dropped almost in the next street on Friday night, but I was below and didn't feel much. I thank God for our shelter. A bomb fell on New St Station one night before we had time to get down, and it was a good old thud. There have been more close to Eileen [south-east Birmingham]. I apparently missed a good go last night [by being at Chedworth] not finishing till 5.45.

At Chedworth we hear planes and faint bombs, but there are no sirens, and it was perfect peace compared to most places. A woman told me in the train that they are trying to get the big junction and railway works at Swindon, but so far have only managed to hit a playing field where a German prison camp is being built . . . Here damage has mainly been done to private property. T.Willetts came in one night in a dazed condition. He works late now and travelled right through a raid. The bus refused to go on; so he got out and apparently walked right into a bomb which knocked him flat. He said the glass fell in two lots, when the bomb fell and then a shower afterwards ahead and behind.

Heaps of our people have had bombs in the garden or windows. I went to see Mrs Whitmore last Wednesday to find a great crater in the road about two minutes off, and she had no gas or water. She said she thought that the house had gone but that the stairs under which they were sheltering were miraculously preserved. One thing she noticed was the crack and crackle of the masonry as it came to pieces. Several people say that. But really life is quite bearable still. I wish more people could enjoy our shelter here.

We walked in the woods most of yesterday – the most marvellous autumn colours . . . The country is extremely beautiful. It was a great relief from town.

Lack of sleep of course, was one of the main miseries of the air raids. At their height a stretch of hours of unbroken sleep seemed the most desirable thing in the world. Workers in the Daily office, generally at such a disadvantage over sleep, now did better than most, for they could go home, even after being imprisoned for hours, and have a morning rest.

Journeys

During the war all sorts of admonitions were dished out to us by poster and advertisement. One that became a catchword was: 'Is your journey really necessary?' Yet people continued to travel as they continued other habits. I had always gone home every four weeks, and I continued to go except for about two months when the London air raids were at their worst.

Trains between Birmingham and London ran as much as they could even through air raids. At the beginning of the raids some of the longest minutes I ever spent were when a train stopped outside Euston. We were told later that part of the track had been bombed, and trains were held up because there were not enough platforms.

But we did not know this. All we knew was that the train had stopped, and twilight, the time for raids to begin, was coming on. I had before me a journey across London, a search at Waterloo for a train to take me out to Surbiton, and then a mile walk. But if I could get to London I could descend to the Underground and so be fairly safe.

But our train did not move, and we were imprisoned. Nobody was about. Nowadays we might have been given some explanation. In those days the policy in breakdowns was to remain out of sight and silent. So we were left stranded as darkness came down.

Nerves worked themselves up into a frenzy until suspense could mount no further and was succeeded by despair. It seemed that the train would never move again; that all trains had stopped for ever. Then, incredibly, after three quarters of an hour, without warning it creaked forward. At Euston the passengers rushed away and I dived

141

for the Underground with the feeling of coming out of a nightmare.

In one way the war increased my journeys, for some people moved out of Birmingham to the country and invited friends to visit them. I went for weekends to Upton-on-Severn, that small Worcestershire town where people had the reputation for politeness. I turned from the town into a lane by fields, and there was nobody about, and presently I saw the blue mass of Malvern brooding in the distance, and it seemed a symbol of peace after all the bombings and murder.

The images on those country visits came with a sharper impact while we were suffering from the war. I shall never forget a line of flowering plum trees at Upton – on a sunny morning with a blue sky behind the mass of white bloom, and all round and above the hum of bees. Another high moment came when I was staying in the cold spring at Chedworth in Gloucestershire famed for its Roman villa – but the villa was lost in the woods and unpublicised then – and I mounted a great green shoulder of hill towards the woods and suddenly heard the cuckoo. But perhaps the most beautiful sight of all was a large purple violet in the hedge, its petals perfectly outlined with a rim of white frost.

Those not working in munition factories continued to have annual holidays. One of the longest journeys I took was from Birmingham to Newquay in Cornwall to stay with a sister's family. In those days one could not be sure of getting to the end of a journey as there might be raids on the way. But we had grown used to uncertainties and just started off and hoped for the best.

One of the things I had not expected was all the bomb stories. As some people like to boast about their illnesses, so these war-time travellers hotly contended for the honour of coming from the most suffering town. The one thing they agreed about was that London had been given too much publicity.

Two soldiers got into the train with me in Birmingham. There had been a raid the night before on New Street Station, and the two had been there and roundly declared that it was worse than anything they had seen in France. The Birmingham passengers looked pleased, but presently we reached the Bristol area, and here a woman got in and declared that no city on earth had been bombed like Bristol. But a passenger from Southampton objected. Everyone, she said, knew that Southampton was the worst hit of all cities. Arguments and bomb stories went on till we reached Cornwall, and then a woman from Truro got in and claimed that the town had had one of the worst raids of the war. She knew nothing of damage done to Birmingham, Bristol or Southampton.

The conversations enlivened the long hours. Darkness fell, and we seemed to be travelling in a no-man's-land. The train's blackout curtains had to be pulled down, and we sat in a confined space isolated from the world. Outside was a solid wall of blackness, and the stations had the merest glimmers of light – without their names which had been taken down when invasion was expected. If one did not know the countryside one was completely lost, but in the war-time atmosphere of friendliness local passengers helped.

I had to change at the small halt of Par. I got down into the blackness with my luggage. I did not know where to go or where my second train would come in. Fortunately I heard voices and asked an unseen figure for directions. I had to cross the line by a bridge, the figure said, and he helped me over in that enormous dark. The journey seemed to take days, but at last I reached Newquay on the Cornish coast. Then, leaving the station, I found one benefit of the blackout – a magnificent sweep of the heavens full of moist golden stars.

But before that, in the May of 1940, I had the oddest journey of all. The German armies were sweeping across Europe, but I had been invited for a week to stay with friends at Nevin in Wales, and I kept to the plan. However, I had to see another friend on the Saturday afternoon; so I went to catch a train at New Street Station in the early evening. The bombing had not yet begun, but train services were uncertain. There was a train going to Conway, but the station officials did not know how long it would take or whether there would be a train going further. 'Take this train and see when you get there,' they said.

At about eleven at night we landed at Conway. In my carriage were a girl with a huge hat, rouged cheeks and jewellery, and two soldiers who were playing truant. The girl watched them and smiled, and they were soon talking. We found that we all wanted to travel south along the Welsh coast. We got out together at Conway and were told that there would be no more trains that night. 'We'll find a taxi,' the soldiers said and disappeared. The girl and I waited. I had no idea how far away Nevin was, but in those days one clung on to any support.

The soldiers returned and said they had found a taxi. The four of us got in at the back, and the soldiers took us on their knees and began to sing loud songs. The car rattled uncertainly along black roads which seemed to have a poor surface, and I tried to feel jolly like the others but could see no end to the adventure. The ride ended abruptly, for the car ran into the parapet of a bridge and stopped. The soldiers jumped out, and looked in again to say that the car was too much damaged to go on any further and in any case the driver was drunk.

We were in the heart of a black countryside. The only thing we could do was to walk on. Presently, at past midnight, we reached a wayside pub. The windows were dark, and there was no-one about; so the soldiers picked up handfuls of gravel and threw it at the windows. Presently a downstairs door opened, and the owner appeared. He did not seem angry, and said he could provide a bed for the girl and me. The soldiers said they had no money and departed to sleep in trucks on the nearby railway.

We were shown into a room with a double bed. The girl, who on closer acquaintance seemed rather dirty, got into bed without washing. I sloshed round a little modestly and climbed into the bed beside her. We must have had a brief sleep, for I became aware of sunlight shining in through a window. We got up and breakfasted amicably together, and I paid for our bed and breakfast. The girl then asked if I could lend her ten shillings – a considerable sum in those days – as she too was short of money. She made a parade of taking my address, and then went off, possibly to join the soldiers. I never heard any more of her.

I set out on a brilliant May Sunday morning to walk five miles to Nevin. It was wonderful to have the night behind me and to be alone, and the hedge banks were full of honeysuckle and pink foxgloves. I finally arrived at my friends' bungalow to find them out. They were astonished when they returned and found me sitting on their doorstep.

That week France fell to the Germans. The bombings and the long years of war lay ahead, but we had a sunny, almost untroubled week in a sandy cleft by the sea. The only differences from usual were queues in the morning outside the one paper shop and Nevin people's decision to cancel their village outing in deference to the fall of France.

War Work

The Lady Mayoress, Mrs Martineau, decided to set the women of Birmingham a good example. The factories could not get enough labour, so she went to work in one herself, with the long hours and manual jobs. She stayed for a fortnight; then decided that she could do more important things.

The women of the kind that I knew in Summer Lane did not need an example. They took jobs not out of patriotism but to get money. Some whose husbands were working in the day on reserved occupations asked to work at night as then there would be someone at home to look after the children. They forgot that they would need to sleep, and they tended to have only catnaps with the baby after the older ones had gone to school. As a result they got hollow-eyed and fatigued.

Presently a network of nurseries was started for the children of working women. At the end of the war it was queried whether the arrangements really helped the war effort much, as nearly as many people were needed to run the nurseries as were released for factory work. But at least the babies got good food and care. And, indeed, the mothers of the children may have been far better at factory work than the baby-carers. Not everyone was suited to a factory job, as I was to find after Dunkirk.

We, the middle-class women, who had not yet been called up, were anxious to be useful. We could help with the WVS and the Citizens' Advice Bureaux, and later there were fire-watching duties. I was barred from the ordinary jobs by my odd working hours, but I did help on one or two Saturdays at the canteen for the Forces that had been set up at New Street Station.

At large stations all over the country ladies were doling out sweets and cigarettes to travelling men. New Street had been bombed and had labour for only essential repairs; so we had a dilapidated room. But there was a counter in front with piled cardboard boxes of chocolate, cakes, biscuits, tea and cigarettes. Much of it was food that we could not buy for ourselves, yet we did not want it. We were there to serve others. We were a sort of angel.

We were very genial to the men who drifted in. If there were only a few we competed for their attention. But often there was a rush and we became hurried and important, hasting to pour out tea and hand out Mars bars. (I had not come across these delicacies before, and thought they were specially aimed at mothers.) Sometimes the men were difficult to understand, and sometimes we got muddled in giving change, but it was a flattering job full of smiles.

But it was not exactly 'vital' – that favourite Civil Service word – war work, and there were other tasks nearer to the nation's effort.

After the withdrawal from Dunkirk, factories making war supplies were ordered to work seven days a week without a break at the weekend. Perhaps it was necessary, though it was found afterwards that when hours were shortened output went up. In any case, workers became fatigued, and at least at one small works the experiment was tried of using volunteers on Sundays.

The Soroptimists recruited volunteers for this scheme, and I joined them for several Sundays. The factory was anxious not to incommode us, and fixed the hours from ten to four-thirty only. To me, with my eccentric sleeping hours, to go to work at ten was like beginning just after midnight, but I was anxious to be useful. It turned out, though, that such anxiety is hardly enough.

The factory was typical of the old Birmingham. In a yard, rickety steps led up to an entrance in a low building of dirty brick. Inside were uneven wooden floors, long benches and overhead belts to feed in the electricity. (These were later condemned for their danger.) The place smelt of machine oil, and we were told that rats were about. Here and there the girls had stuck up small bits of mirrors, but there were no proper cloakrooms.

When we arrived two or three factory bosses were there. We stood by a table and were divided into groups for different jobs. I was in the screw group. The screws came to us with flat ends as they had been cut off from longer rods, and we had to give them points by grinding them against a revolving wheel. It sounded simple but proved difficult – for me at any rate. We had to make our points into even cones and to keep our fingers away from the wheel – neither of which I did. Sparks of metal flew off the wheel, and the benches were full of noise and heat.

The trouble with the bosses was that they were too polite. They went round inspecting our efforts and courteously again showed us how to do the work properly. Some of the regular workers had come in with the amateurs, and we had only to glance at them to see how incapable we were. They sang, chatted above the noise of the machinery, fluffed out their hair, chewed sweets – and with an expert flick turned out a series of perfectly finished screws. They must have done twice as many as we did.

A quarter of an hour before the bull (hooter) sounded for the lunchbreak they stopped work and began to comb their hair and powder before their one large mirror. On the first day I struggled on, conscious of my poor harvest. 'You work too hard,' one of the girls said kindly, and she switched off the electricity so that I could not do any more. She would have laughed if she could have seen my screws.

We ate our sandwiches of peanut butter – to save the butter ration – on the premises, and presently the machines were switched on again. The afternoon seemed long, yet we finished at half-past four. Then we lined up and were given eight shillings each, generous pay for those days.

I had thought that during the work I could do some concentrated thinking, but I found this impossible. Just enough thought was needed for the work to inhibit an escape to other meditations. No wonder factory girls were not interested in culture.

I also ground a finger on the wheel, and the heat made a permanent scar. Then I got a fragment of metal, a spark from the wheel, in my eye. It did not hurt much but I could not get it out. When I went into the office the next day the printers made a fuss about it, and finally Wag walked me down to Birmingham Eye Hospital. An expert picked out the fragment in a second, but I was ashamed of being a nuisance. After that I wore goggles.

The trouble about the job was that you worked only once a week, and in between Sundays forgot any skill that you had acquired. I must have been one of the worst grinders, but we must have been generally unsatisfactory, for our polite employers presently found that our work did not justify the trouble of organising us. So the scheme was quietly dropped.

I made one more attempt to help my country by voluntary work. We were told that farmers, who had to provide more food because of the submarines round our shores, were desperate for labour. I was going to stay for a week with the Mrs M.-H. who had entertained me for years at her large house at Harborne. She had moved out to Upton, and said she would arrange with a farmer for me to work on the land.

I associated Upton with meadows sloping to the river and a pear tree, brilliant with white blossom, that dazzled one in spring by the path to the house. I had a vague idea, fed by all those books on the country of the last fifty years, that rural people were superior to town ones. But I was disappointed.

I started work on a breezy not too hot summer morning – quite inviting, one might have thought, to labourers. My job was to pull out two in every three young mangolds sown in lines in a vast field – leaving, of course, the best plants to grow on. The job meant continual stooping, and presently I began to ache all over. A middle-aged farm hand was working with me, and we conversed amiably now and then. We stopped at twelve for lunch; had about three quarters of an hour sitting by a hedge and then went on till four.

My countryman surprised me. I had thought he would know the names of all the flowers and birds of the Worcestershire field, but he seemed to know few names, and made remarks such as, 'them little things are always about.' He used his eyes, however, for the matters that concerned him. He knew what the weather was going to be by the clouds that came over, and he told the time for the midday break by a milk cart that rattled down the lane far down the field.

When I got out of bed the next day I was so stiff that I could hardly walk, but I went back to the field. That afternoon I returned to find that my hostess had gone to her afternoon rest and locked the door; so I lay on the lawn in front of the house and myself fell asleep. After a day or so I ceased to ache and worked better. But then the field was finished and I was not wanted any more.

These little jobs changed my ideas about the dignity of labour. Each manual task is very unimportant as the Lady Mayoress had found. Also, you cannot think great thoughts while you are grinding screws or pulling up mangolds. The more we can get machines to work for us the better.

Factory Meeting

One afternoon when I was looking over a factory I met a woman and two men. They had south country accents like mine, and they seemed persons of authority, for they were received with great politeness. Then I was told that they were from the Ministry of Labour, and had come to talk over some problem. I knew nothing of ministries, but as visitors we were drawn together, and we left the factory at the same time and took a tram into the centre of town.

We talked after we had left the tram, and they told me about the straits of their ministry. It needed staff desperately as its work had expanded so enormously. And now more work was coming, for all women under fifty who had no young children were to be called up and put into war jobs. Educated women were vitally – again that word – needed to conduct the interviews.

These Ministry of Labour people pricked my conscience. If women were needed so desperately surely I should not be sitting in a newspaper office. I asked if anybody like myself would be useful.

Yes certainly, they said affably, and they gave me an address to write to. 'Mention, if you like, that you have met us.'

I went back to the office and told Mr R. that women were needed desperately by the Ministry of Labour. This time he did not object to my temporary departure. His staff was elderly and was not in danger of being called up, and the Daily, with the rationing of paper, had grown much smaller. He would allow me to be seconded to the ministry, and the firm would pay me a retaining fee of £50 a year. My departure would be only short, for we had already had more than eighteen months of war. And meanwhile I could also write articles for the leader page, which every day had a column essay.

'But stay here till they call you,' Mr R. said genially. 'Don't hurry away.'

I did not hurry away. The Ministry of Labour did not allow me to. Two weeks passed and there was no answer to my letter offering my services. I had expected an answer by return. I did not know my ministries in those days. However, after a fortnight a reply did come on dauntingly thin and ugly brownish paper. I was told later that this was a really quick response.

But it said only that my 'request for employment' was being considered. Slightly taken aback, I waited on. Then another ugly-looking communication arrived. I was offered the post of Third Class Officer, whatever that was, at a salary of £280 a year.

The smallness of the salary surprised me, but money had been coming in so abundantly through the years that it had ceased to be important to me. I felt virtuous in taking a salary of about half what I was earning, but then I wanted to be useful. I wished the Ministry of Labour would be a little grateful for my sacrifice, but perhaps a certain coldness was part of a government office. I was to realise later that a very small salary meant a low status and little responsibility.

Nor did I know then anything about the pyramid system by which a third-class officer was supervised by a second-class officer, and a second-class officer by a first-class officer and so on. By the system, I was to find, you might not go to anybody but the officer next above you so that your affairs and sometimes protests got muted and changed as they went up the ladder. Actually I did sometimes go above my amiable second-class officer, but afterwards I thought I should never forget these grades and their complications; but I have.

I wrote to the ministry at once and accepted. I would have

accepted anything. Then I was told to report at the ministry's headquarters in the late spring of 1941.

In the Daily office I wrote my last war work article and cleared out my desk. I came across layer after layer from the past – postcards from the madman, invitations to tea parties, articles which had been sent without addresses, thanks for my own articles. Dusty and faded, most of the relics went into the wastepaper bin. For the first time in ten years my drawers were empty.

I left some rubber rings and paper clips for the future. I kept a very few papers and put them on top of the big account books, no longer needed, in the cupboard. I did not say any formal goodbyes. I should still be coming in to look for post, and with my retaining fee I should still be part of the office. I had never been in Birmingham and not part of the Daily.

But I did not realise the changes that four years can bring.

First Day

I was so much afraid of being late that first morning that I arrived three quarters of an hour early – at something after eight. The ministry headquarters was a towering red building at the impoverished end of Corporation Street and fixed on one side to a public house as I was to find to my cost later. On its bottom floor it incorporated an employment exchange – we were not to use the derogatory term 'labour exchange' I was early informed – and it was policy for the ministry to site its exchanges away from classy districts as the queues might annoy people and cause comment.

Inside, it was just a collection of one corridor over another, all almost alike, with a cloakroom at the end. The top was different as it had the canteen. At the beginning I used to forget which corridor I was in, but presently, as with so much at the ministry, I grew accustomed to them.

On my arrival the doorman said he knew nothing of my coming – a change from the effusive welcome that I usually received. He ushered me into a cold bare waiting-room near the door, and there I was left to hear many people passing but none for me. Time went on. Now and then I emerged to ask that a message might go to the man who had written to me, but nothing happened. I was there till after eleven.

At last somebody came and looked in at the door. I was conducted up dark steps to a small bare room where an apologetic man behind a desk greeted me. And in all the pettiness and constraints of that office there was one thing that would stand out – the mildness and good temper of all those officers, first, second and third class. They too suffered under the system, which made for jealousy and took away initiative, but they almost never did an ill-tempered thing. There were dozens of bulging files to convict them if they ever lost their tempers.

I had expected to become an interviewer of women who were called up, but instead I was to be the subject of a great experiment – a 'publicity officer'. The agreeable man explained that the Ministry of Information was supposed to do publicity work for the Ministry of Labour but had not been – well – 'entirely satisfactory'. This was my first intimation that government departments dislike one another. So I was, at £280 a year, to publicise the Ministry of Labour in the Midlands.

He implied that it was a breath-taking decision – another intimation, this time, of the enormous importance the office attached to small matters. Civil Servants, he said, were trained to silence, and so they would not be happy in issuing information. And indeed I was soon to notice this dread of saying anything for fear of being found out in some way. And I was not to worry, he concluded, if I had not a lot to do at first.

So I was introduced to one of the chief burdens at Divisional Office, later to change its name, after weighty discussions, to Regional Office – idleness. In spite of what my previous informants had said, there were too many of us at RO, and a large number of us had not enough to do. It was partly that we were small cogs in a vast machine and partly 'empire building'. The larger the staff under an officer the more likely he was to win promotion. So he talked of the 'vital necessity' of having more staff, and more girls would be brought in. And they would have little to do except go on messages, put papers in files and take round the attendance book and morning and afternoon tea. So they would spend long minutes in the women's cloakroom combing their hair and talking.

I did not spend hours in the cloakroom. I tried to make jobs for myself, but it was difficult. Other people freely admitted that they had not much to do, but said that work came in waves and they would be swamped with it later. And of course there were always training courses to mop up idleness. The Ministry of Labour had a

151

great respect for education, and arranged training for counter staff of exchanges. This occupied both staff and trainers. But the training did not seem of brilliant quality as I noticed later when I uncomfortably shared a room with some trainers.

But all this was far ahead. 'We are finding you a secretary,' the kind man said.

'I don't need a secretary,' I said.

'To keep the files, to liaise with the typing pool.'

'But I always do my own typing.'

'Oh, that wouldn't be allowed here. We have our own typing grade.'

He would find me a corner to sit, the nice man said, and later a room. I could begin that afternoon by reading through files and circulars.

The files that somebody brought me were cream covers bulging with untidy papers devoted to different subjects – mainly a few 'drives' in co-operation with the Ministry of Information. Files were the life blood of RO, and we all had special metal filing cabinets. The file was supposed to tell the story of an action from beginning to end. If you wanted to know something you did not ask the person concerned. You asked for the file. So not a shred of paper – not even 'Please see me' – might be thrown away, and every paper must be dated, and the date had to be in a certain corner. The files made work for dozens of little clerks who put in the papers and carried them about. Only when an action was over could you 'close' a file.

The circulars were leaflets or booklets printed on thin cheap paper with semi-legal language which was often obscure. RO staff suspected that the begetters left their meaning unclear so that later, if things went wrong, they could say that they did not mean what they appeared to say. One woman officer told me that she thought of the circular-writers as spiders in some dark London den spinning out their webs. Each circular seemed to refer to another such as C.24 or X10, and these in turn referred to other circulars. I read a number with my best attention that first afternoon, but simply could not take them in – and when I did they did not seem to be saying much.

The afternoon seemed endless, but we emerged from the gaunt cold building at five. I went down to the Daily office, and it was strange to find that the evening staff had not yet arrived. I collected a few letters and went home.

I recognised afterwards that I had been spoilt in my previous job. Also ministries were no doubt different in peace time. When I criticised the system to permanent staff they said, 'It was different before all you temporaries came in. Of course there's some confusion with all these extra people and work.' All the same, a number of the new little clerks left through boredom and joined the Forces, and one Oxford graduate, described as 'brilliant' by the ministry which so much revered education, resigned from a fairly high position after the war.

The others did not go. 'Once you've got into the system you can't leave. No one would take you.' And then, of course, they knew they were safe and would have a pension at the end.

I had thought that all temporaries would be horrified at RO, but one, much respected, who had been brought in to arrange lodgings in Birmingham for workers from other areas, told me after the war, to my surprise, that she had plenty of work and a good time. All the same, when I was sent to meet her, we spent most of the afternoon laughing at the ways of Regional Office.

Jobs

'You must get to know our employment exchanges,' my second-class officer said. So I did a round of visits throughout the region, from Leamington Spa, where there was the one woman exchange manager in the region, to Stoke-on-Trent. Each time I was given a character sketch of the man or woman I was going to see, for these ministry people, who had to be anonymous in their work, loved to gossip about one another's characters.

The grades of the managers varied according to the importance of their exchanges. In this time of much employment of women they all had a woman in charge of the female side. The women were of a lower grade but generally – as in Regional Office – better educated than the men. When I visited the exchanges I usually saw both and got a cup of tea somewhere. For as Regional Office bowed with intense respect before London headquarters, so the exchanges bowed before Regional Office. I used to think there was a terrible amount of kow-towing.

The exchanges were generally down sordid side streets and kept as much as possible out of sight of the affluent public. An attempt was being made to rescue them from the harsh reputation they had had in the past, and they were adorned with posters, and some of the women had flowers in their rooms. But always one had the same impression, as indeed one had to Regional Office, of cheapness, bareness, a lack of all the graces of life.

In my visits the managers talked about the difficulties of their areas. The chief problem was nearly always shortage of labour. Another, they generally said, was their own overwork. Regional Office had not much idea of real work, they implied, while they were overburdened, but they would not be at RO for anything.

The idea of making employment exchanges attractive to the public did not succeed. People continued to call them 'labour exchanges' and associate them with the working classes. In the end separate centres were opened for the 'gentry'.

I had many interesting conversations at the employment exchanges, but my visits were hardly a help in winning the war. Possibly another of my early activities was a little more useful. With a flutter of triumph I was told that a band of women journalists from London was coming to Birmingham to visit factories. Their itinerary had been worked out, but I was to book their hotel rooms and go with them and explain things.

My officers were all excitement over these women. In the past I had been given exaggerated respect as a journalist. Now I was expected to feel the same admiring wonder. I had become an official, answering the naive questions of this smart group who, as so often in journalism, were going to write articles when they knew almost nothing about the subject.

There was one older, fatter, less elegant woman among them. She was not as anxious to be agreeable and she left early. But afterwards she produced the most intelligent article of them all. She was from *The Times*.

I was also supposed to answer questions from the public generally. There were not very many of these, as most people had no idea that the Ministry of Labour had a Regional Office, and they took their queries to the employment exchanges. But once a man who had had to fill in a long form' wrote asking why a certain question which seemed irrelevant was asked. I sent his letter down to the employment exchange on our premises, and after a time a reply came back from the manager. He did not know and never had known why the question was asked.

I enquired once what happened to all the forms that were filled in, sometimes in triplicate. My informant said they 'went into a cupboard'. At the time Churchill was sending out a message to civil servants telling them to cut down the paperwork, but the message seemed to have no effect on us.

Apropos of questions from the public, this same exchange manager told me that when he was asked a difficult question he did not answer for a fortnight. 'By that time,' he said, 'the need for answering it has generally passed.'

Another of my functions was to help run publicity campaigns. Before I joined the department the Ministry of Information had arranged a few appeals to women to do war work, and these perhaps had some use. But when I arrived women up to fifty were being called up and compulsorily put into war work so that the time for appeals had gone. But the machine, having started up, went on turning. Of course there were still women over fifty and mothers of young children who were not being compelled to work. We might touch their hearts. But our harvest got smaller and smaller.

The process would begin with one of the exchange managers reporting a special shortage of labour in his area. Some factory had taken on new assignments. The position changed all the time and emergencies were frequent. There would be a consultation. What about a campaign? The manager would be pleased. Unfortunately the Ministry of Information must be brought in.

After more discussions it would be decided to invite Ministry of Information representatives to a meeting at RO. Say at ten o'clock. So three of them would come, and there would be about seven of us altogether. At eleven cups of tea would be brought in. A certain jargon would go about. Could So-and-So 'cope'? Would So-and-So 'play ball'? The words 'vital' and 'appropriate' were used many times.

There were two ardent young women at the Ministry of Information who were probably under-employed as I was and wanted to take the affair over. One particularly did most of the talking. But it was the Ministry of Labour's campaign, and we were paying for it. So eventually action was divided – and the whole morning had gone. After the meeting I had to write reports to officers who might be interested, and there were several of them.

I used to like those meetings. They made me feel necessary. Later on the Ministry of Information did not obtrude so much and I planned posters and wrote leaflets on my own. There was a great relief in dealing with the printers. The kindly old head of the firm would come in to see me, and I would feel that for a moment I was back in the real outside world.

One meeting, however, caused me a trivial sense of humiliation which I think many of those anonymous lower orders felt. It had been large, outside Birmingham, and a Ministry of Information man, who with me laughed now and then at the ways of government departments, had motored me out. The meeting, however, seemed to go quite well, and I thought no more of it till one of my superior officers told me that Miss S. had complained of something I had said.

Miss S. was our star lady, aged about forty, already a first-class officer. She was later to be promoted to principal. I knew little about her except that she was very friendly with one of the office men and probably got her satisfaction from work and his companionship. We had exchanged a few polite words.

What had I said to annoy Miss S.? My officer did not know. She had not specified; only said that the remark was inappropriate. I asked other people who had been at the meeting. They did not know. I never did find out what the offending words were.

Miss S. was a high-ranking officer. Did she have to bother about trifles? And if she did, why had she not come to me? Perhaps these amiable ministry people never did risk direct confrontation. It was all very silly, but in a country weekend I sat in a peaceful field and could not enjoy it because I was angry. I never spoke to Miss S. again.

To make myself more of a job I began to write small inspiring pieces for local newspapers. My articles were supposed to encourage people to support the war effort. Rather in the old Russian style I found heroes among the workers – people in key positions, disabled people who did full-time work.

In the free old days I had typed articles, and they had gone straight up to the printers. Now I had to write the articles out and give them to my girl, who took them through long corridors to the typists' pool. This had a dragon of a lady in charge, and she often said she had no typist free. There were, however, some charming girls among the typists who always got the work done as soon as they could.

But then I had to take the stuff to my superior officer, who admitted that he was 'a bloke without much education'. The ministry was very keen on correct English, and I was told the story of a man who wrote a letter beginning 'I presume'. The officer above him crossed out 'presume' and wrote in 'assume'. The man above him went back to 'presume', and the letter went through four changes before it was sent. Whether 'presume' or 'assume' won in the end I was not told.

My own officer objected to small points. In one note on a worker I had written 'his factory'. Should it not be, Mr H. asked, 'the factory in which he works'? 'His factory' implied that he owned the place. The newspapers were pressed for space and I resisted him; and on this occasion he retreated.

But my notes for local papers landed me in the worst trouble I ever had at Regional Office. It was all about nothing and yet it might have led to questions in Parliament – the most awful fate that Regional Office could imagine.

An employment exchange had written that there was an interesting man who might be interviewed at a local factory. I went out and found a limping worker who had come from Germany. He had been taken prisoner but had been so badly wounded that he had been repatriated under the Red Cross.

In those war years people who had been used to visiting the continent regularly had, I think, a feeling of claustrophobia. We felt boxed in. We did not know what was happening over there. So I possibly questioned extra-eagerly this man who had come from Germany. He had been in hospital there for some months, and told me that the people were quite nice and he had been kindly treated.

This news was a relief after all the propaganda. Possibly I wanted to raise a small voice of moderation. But if I did it was very, very small, for all I said was that a German hospital had treated this wounded prisoner kindly, and he had found people quite nice.

My officer was out that afternoon. 'Oh, send it off,' he had said when I told him that I had a screed for him to read. I sent it.

Early in the morning a few days later my telephone began to ring from London. Several papers seemed anxious to know my views on Germany. One hectoring voice that came back twice wanted to know if I was fond of the Germans. Did I or did I not agree that 'the only good German is a dead 'un'? In the end I said, 'I don't know what you mean,' and rang off.

Then my second-class officer sent a girl. Had I got a copy of my article and any files connected with it? So I sent the copy and an untidy file, and for a short time there was silence.

By then I was aware that I had committed some frightful fault though I did not know what. I sank deeper into apprehension when a message came that I was to answer no more telephone calls from London but to have them transferred to a superior officer.

Some days later somebody did explain what was the matter. The trouble had come from the *Daily Worker*, the Communist paper which was still attacking the Government. The *Daily Worker* had had a correspondent in south France where fighting was going on, and he had been so antagonistic to the command that he had been ordered home. Now the paper was taking its revenge.

Someone had seen the mild little local article and passed it to the *Daily Worker*. The paper had published a story that, while workers in Birmingham were labouring night and day for the war effort, some woman in the local headquarters of the Ministry of Labour was putting out propaganda for the Germans. My one half sentence about the hospital being kind was quoted out of context.

London headquarters had read the *Daily Worker* and had demanded information. This was the worst possible thing that could happen to Regional Office, always so subservient to London authority. And then there might be the awful sequel of questions in Parliament.

I looked at my article again. The affair was laughable. Nobody in his senses could have objected to half a sentence saying that a German hospital was kind. And yet somehow this storm had blown up.

On this occasion I admired the secret working of the ministry. There was silence from my officers; no shouting as there might have been in a newspaper office. RO parleyed with London and I was glad at being treated as a child and spared embarrassment. Then the affair ended. Questions in Parliament were avoided. I was only told gently not to mention Germany again in my articles.

I expected to be removed from my job. Instead, a little later, the important statement was made that my name was to be changed. There had been discussions at headquarters. There was need to fall into line with other ministries. It was all a matter of great weight.

What was the important decision? In future I was not to be called 'publicity officer' but 'public relations officer'.

Would it alter my grade? No. Would it alter the work? No. All the same it was a 'vitally' important change.

So the so-called work went on and I still arranged campaigns, little response as we got to them. Sometimes the aim was almost impossible – how for example to get women outside the call-up ages to go and work in pottery factories in north Staffordshire. They were needed for war contracts, but the pottery industry had always paid low wages, while there was an ROF (Royal Ordnance Factory) near where the women earned large wages. The only inducement to the pottery work that could be offered to the very few women available was specially arranged part-time hours and the nearness of the factories to their homes.

And if nobody much responded I had found a new dodge. An employment exchange manager had once told me that volunteers sometimes came forward months after a campaign had finished. So I could hint at future results.

There was one advantage in these activities. I had to write reports for a number of officers, and this occupied time. I also had to write a short weekly report and a longer monthly report on what I was doing, and report-writing was a way of using up empty hours.

One thing I learned – always to keep some little job in hand so that I did not come in in the morning with absolutely nothing to do. But oh, the pleasure when I arrived in the morning to find an envelope or an instruction on my desk.

Discomforts

Regional Office stood high in a wide street where winds always seemed to blow. When you entered after being buffeted you went into darkness except for the sparkles from the composition steps. There was a lift to the upper corridors, but it seemed to be frequently out of order because it was maintained by the Ministry of Works which was busy. In any case you did not ring up another ministry when you wanted something, but wrote your request on a docket, and that took time. The Ministry of Works also shared the cleaning of the grimy cream-coloured walls. Ministry of Labour cleaners did as high as they could reach without ladders, while Works was responsible for the upper part, which was always dirty.

The rooms were bare and anonymous with cheap desks, filing cabinets, perhaps a shelf or two of official publications and brown linoleum. Higher-ranking officials were given a carpet, a sign of the general worship of rank. One of the first things I noticed when I joined RO was the obsequiousness to higher officials. Once I was talking to my first-class officer when he opened a drawer and took out a duster. With this he vigorously dusted his shoes. The reason? An official from London was coming that afternoon.

A linked discomfort for the soul was the emphasis on promotion, which was partly, no doubt, dependent on the money available. A man who was disgruntled at lack of promotion told me that the best way to get on was to 'ear-ole', suck up to, one's superiors. But it must have been difficult to decide on promotions, for all the sections seemed to work separately, quite unaware of what the others were doing.

When you were promoted you were moved to some quite different job. You might be a wizard of finance but you were shifted to 'training' or 'lodgings', often in another part of the country. RO was full of people from the north and Yorkshire, which incidentally made it more interesting.

One man told me that his children had been to six different schools. If you were unwilling to move you did not get promotion.

When we arrived in the morning we were presented with a large attendance book, ruled in red after nine o'clock, to be signed. The little girls brought round the books, which gave them something to do. But though we were in by nine it did not necessarily mean that we started work then. The men were known to sign the book and then go out to get a haircut.

We would settle down to what work there was to do, the little girls curling their pretty hair round their fingers, sorting papers, putting them in files and going from the room for long periods, ostensibly on messages. But in mid-morning and mid-afternoon they became cherubim. For then would come the rumble of the tea trolley for which we had been listening for half an hour, and they would run out and crowd round the trolley like bees round a honey pot. Back they would come with steaming cups, the tea rather stewed but hot enough to put warmth into our veins. For a few minutes we could sip and break off from whatever dull job we were doing. No wonder tea has become a joke in the Civil Service.

My various secretaries included one or two charmingly pretty girls, but they grew bored. They were shifted about in the continual changes of staff, and some left. At one time I had a willing and pleasant housewife of over forty drafted in with the call-up of women. She was obviously not suitable for a little clerk's job, and I did not like to ask her to run on messages. At the end I had Ivy, past her first youth and with a strong Birmingham accent but pious and sensible. She used to regale us with stories of her father, who had a fish stall in the Bull Ring. One of its drawbacks was the awful smell of his clothes.

I changed rooms as often as I changed secretaries. As promised I had a small separate room at the beginning, but new people were constantly being brought in, and the room was soon wanted for somebody else. We were then shifted to a den of smoke at the end of a corridor. The source of the smoke was the chimney of the pub next door. It had never been properly insulated, and when the wind was in the south or west clouds of smoke filtered in to Regional Office. On the wall by the chimney a great wad of paper had been stuck, one paper over the other to keep out the smoke – yellow newspapers slapped on, we imagined, by a series of occupants. We stuck more newspaper on top, but still the smoke came through. Even when we left our door open we could sometimes hardly breathe, and clothes and papers picked up the smoke smell.

We asked if something could be done about the room, but it was impossible. The Ministry of Works was responsible here as well, and the Ministry of Works was busy with important things.

But we did not stay long. Still more people came in, and we could not expect a room of our own. While the authorities were looking for a corner for us, we were put at the end of a long room where a number of people were working. There was continuous noise with much walking to and fro, but worse was a fiendish draught blasting down on our heads. I had suffered from earache in my youth, and I was afraid of draughts. I asked if we could be moved again, but all I got was a rickety screen which was not much good at keeping out the blast.

However, presently one of my officers assured me that a very good niche had been found for us. We were to share a room with three ladies arranging training courses for the clerks. The ladies would be out a good deal of the time.

The ladies were seldom out, and the three of them spent most of their time talking, for they too had not enough to do. An effort was being made to train the girls at employment exchanges in politeness. They were not to bawl down the counter, 'Here's a woman of thirty-seven wanting a job,' but be careful about publicising ages and courteous to enquirers. This was, of course, very commendable, but from our point of view it was not preached in classes often enough. So the ladies stayed in RO and sat and talked.

How do you convey to people that their conversations are interrupting you? At first I tried being silent myself. Then the ladies forgot that we were there, and conversation flowed even more merrily. So I tried another tack – phone calls. You could always think of someone whom you should phone. Directly you raised your voice the conversation down the room ceased and they all listened. The phone calls quietened the noise for a time, and sometimes I escaped by being out in the afternoon.

Another source of intense discomfort was the heating rules. They were fixed by date for Government offices, and periods of misery were late autumn before the heating was switched on and early spring when it was switched off. In the cold one grew too stiff to move. Some people brought in hot-water bottles. I swathed myself in a motoring rug. In the lunch hour one walked to generate a hint of warmth.

Almost with delight we returned to work on the Monday that heating was to go on. But it was a stuffy sort of heat and tended to make you sleepy. In my first winter I brought in a bowl of daffodil bulbs to cheer the grimy bareness. The leaves grew at a great rate – taller and taller till they looked like grass. After a time they dropped over and yellowed. There were no flowers. I did not try again.

There were no cafés near that desolate end of Corporation Street; so most of us used the canteen at the top of RO. You could warm up a little there and you did not have to give up any ration tickets. But the helpings must have been small, for we were advised to eat slowly as this would make us feel fuller. Towards the end of the war several of us got into the habit of going across bombed wastes to a small bread shop and buying any buns that it had. Bread and cake were not rationed till after the war. We carried the bag of dry buns back and handed them round the room as an addition to lunch.

RO stood so high that it should have had a good view from the top storeys. But it looked out over the dirty brick wastes of Aston, where now there were spreading ruins from bombing. The only modern building was the large Birmingham Fire Station across the way. The view had absolutely nothing to give pleasure to the eye until one day we noticed that a large space near the Fire Station was being flattened by heavy machinery. The job went on for days, and none of us had any idea what it was for. It looked like a preparation for tennis courts, but we hardly thought that firemen in wartime would play tennis in their spare time. At last one day we saw that the enclosure was being filled with water. A large reservoir had been made to ensure supplies in raids, though now these were slackening. From that time one could look out and see the water reflecting the sky, and that was one refuge in all the ugliness within and without.

But once I had a strange view that must be very rare. We had to take turns to fire-watch in RO at weekends, and one Sunday I was on duty with an acquaintance lost in the bowels of the vast building. It was winter, but we had summer time then, and as I came in at 8.30 it was still dark but with a brilliant moon shining. It was a morning of showers, and as I looked out of my high window rain came pouring down. Then I saw something I did not know existed – a moon rainbow. It was slighter and less vivid than the sun type, but it arched the dark with a silvery radiance. It was ghostly and ethereal and startling, but it did not last long.

Presently our day at RO was extended. Some critic pointed out that, while factories were working enormously long hours, civil servants were still leaving at five. An edict went out that we must stay till six, but at the same time nobody was given any more to do. Some of the men worked till just after five and then went up to the canteen and had toast and dripping till six o'clock.

For most of my first year at the ministry I was paid only about four pounds a month. When, somewhat aghast, I asked about this pittance, I was told that the Civil Service was paying tax a year ahead of the ordinary public. The two systems were to be brought together, and finally the ordinary public came into the Civil Service system, but was forgiven the extra year's tax.

Those who entered the Civil Service in the war would have to pay two years' tax to bring them into line. They would, however, be compensated after the war. Meanwhile my salary, with income tax deducted at the source, would continue to be four pounds a month till I had paid off the two years. I had, of course, previously earned a good salary and now was earning a poor one, and this accounted for some of my loss of income.

So I kept myself on savings, on the Daily's fifty pounds a year and money from an occasional article. I was never compensated after the war, as had been promised, because of some quibble about the Daily's retaining fee. Meanwhile I was left with a faint sense of resentment. But then many people in RO had that.

The World Outside

When one was in Regional Office one felt completely cut off from the world outside the Ministry of Labour. Similarly, after I had left, the great red building, with its disciplined hordes, dropped away almost as though it had never been.

But in those war days there was still some escape at weekends, and I used part of them on research for articles for the Daily. I had always worked on Midland history, and I went on with that, if possible linking it with anniversaries or topical occasions. One had only to go to Birmingham Central Library to discover the large number of well-known people who had connections with the Midlands. I wrote about Dr John Dee, rector at Upton-on-Severn, the scientist and wizard of the reign of Elizabeth I; about Rowland Hill, begetter of the penny post, whose family had had a school at Edgbaston; about Matthew Arnold who had visited the city and walked along Hagley Road.

On Saturday afternoons I sat in the Victorian gloom of the library and returned to my old Birmingham. In spite of the war the library had vases of flowers, and I remember one great golden chrysanthemum sparkling in the electric light. Such sights were unknown in our gaunt RO. There was one thing that particularly surprised me about Birmingham Library – the enormous hoards of papers that had never been examined or described, tempting collections shut away and unknown. One could have written dozens of books on them. There was, for example, a huge collection of letters from Josiah Wedgwood. But books on Wedgwood were not wanted at the time, and I had no leisure.

I saw old friends at the weekends. Their lives had generally been changed less than mine, but we all, of course, were affected by wartime shortages. I used to go out fortnightly to a family at Hall Green and take small presents to the two boys. There came a time when there was absolutely nothing to buy for them except paper trifles, and their mother earnestly asked me not to waste my money on any more 'muck'.

Sometimes I went in the old way to see my printer friend Pimmy at Yardley. I could not tell him much about the Ministry of Labour, and he would not have been much interested; so we talked of old times and the Daily office. This was no longer cheerful. Among the printers Bert, Tom and Bill had been called up, and Harold's son had been killed over Germany. The Daily was very thin, as paper was severely rationed. Everybody was 'just carrying on and waiting for the end'.

But then there was a devastating series of deaths. Mr R., our talkative editor, sickened and died in hospital. Sir Charles, the munificent owner of the Daily group, died, and then Ned, the chief reporter who used to look at photographs with me, died, and finally Wag, the head printer who had been so much part of my life. The paper began to seem like a ship without a captain.

I used to go to my room in the Daily office sometimes on Saturday afternoons to write my articles. After all, I was only seconded to the

Ministry of Labour. The return reminded me of old days – the warren of a building, dark, warm and empty, only a watchman at the side door. But presently I noticed, without paying much attention, signs of other occupation – an ashtray, another paper tray, discarded newspapers in the bin.

One afternoon I walked in to find a bald-headed middle-aged reporter sitting at my desk. He had been friendly in the old days, and had occasionally embarrassed me by offering articles which were not very brilliant. He had been considered only a mediocre reporter, but now he looked at me with a stony eye and said it was his room.

I heard later that, with shortage of staff, he was being tried as a leader writer and so was installed on the landing. It turned out, I heard, that he was not equal to the job, but that afternoon I did not dispute his claim. I left at once, feeling banished, and did not try to use the room again. I had had, however, the arrangement with Mr R. about the retaining fee and my return at the end of the war. There was nothing in writing, but the firm was still paying me the fifty pounds annually. I had, I thought, only to wait.

My old friend, L.P.H., the leader writer, at last was appointed editor. I went to see him one evening, but it was like talking to a stranger. He seemed much older, not very friendly and vague about my future. 'You must wait till the war is over,' he said. Soon after that he too died.

Last Months

The last year or so at RO was in some ways the most comfortable. Almost every person who could do work was doing it, but we still out of habit arranged small publicity campaigns and I still wrote about noble war workers. I had learned the habits of the place; kept every scrap of paper to go into our monster files; took a deep interest in promotion and wondered if I should ever become a second-class officer – but I never did – and liked many of the staff. But the best thing was the waiting for the war to end. We were all waiting. Peace had become a sort of Garden of Eden.

Life was also made pleasanter by Mr B. who arrived as a principal and one of the bosses of RO. He had been the manager of a large flourishing employment exchange by the Thames, and was known as a vigorous and unconventional figure. He had perhaps been sent to us because the Midlands were playing a large part in making equipment for the D-day landings, still a secret. He surprised me from the beginning. One could really talk to him as an independent human being and forget officers and grades. He was genial, and he had been in touch with the outside world.

Mr B. began to hold Monday morning meetings in his room. He noticed, as I had, that there were all the different sections doing things unknown to one another, and the meetings were to let representatives realise what was going on generally; to give them a picture of the situation.

I was not one of the high-up officers, but he invited me to come too. This had two benefits. I had something definite to do when I arrived on Monday, and I saw the general movement of labour, and the work at RO began to take on some meaning.

In the early spring of 1944 we were told that workers were being recruited – I think for Wales – to make some sort of harbour. The matter was deadly secret. We were not to say a word. For months the rumours of some invasion of France had been going about. Now we knew it was a reality. As the weeks went on there were more veiled references to some great buildup.

The spring of 1944 was very stormy, and it seemed to the public that nothing was happening except air raids over Germany and rocket bombs from the Germans falling on London. Through April and May people waited, and no invasion took place. 'Nothing is going to happen after all,' people said in Birmingham. But the RO knew better.

One June morning I came to my room as usual and signed the attendance book. Then one of the men poked his head in at the door and said, 'They've invaded.' The news had been on the wireless that morning. Immediately the world changed. We dropped our papers and began to talk, and all that day, with people looking in and passing on the frequent radio bulletins, the excitement and comradeship continued.

Afterwards the war took longer to end than we had expected, but we were fed by news of continual victories and 'liberations' and we realised that we had only to wait. Regional Office had a radio in a room at the end of one corridor, and some of the men used to assemble there to listen to the six o'clock news. I had no radio at home, and used to go along too. We were all excited, and grades were forgotten, and we talked like human beings. The whole of RO seemed more homelike.

Excitement followed excitement. One evening as I passed the churchyard the cathedral bells began to peal. I knew what it was for. The Allies had at last entered Paris, and this was a peal of joy. I went home feeling that the long sickening years were over, but actually the celebration was premature, as the allies held back to allow General do Gaulle to enter first, and this did not happen till the next day.

Once when I was walking down Corporation Street at the end of the day I saw a crowd of people on the other side of the road. They were outside the office of the Daily's old rival group of papers, and I was told by a passer-by that horror pictures of Belsen, which the Allies had just entered, had been fixed on boards outside. I did not cross, but I noticed that the crowd was pushing round the photographs with a ghoulish fascination. Since our forces had been in Germany and in contact with the ordinary people, the old cry that 'the only good German is a dead 'un' had disappeared. It was even reported in the papers that the German people seemed friendly. Yet now, it appeared, we were all degraded by horrors, including the newspaper that had put the photographs out as a popular attraction and the people who responded.

But it was not the time to lament over the growth of sadism. In the spring of 1945 we could be content. Blackout rules were lifted. The rocket bombs no longer plagued the south. Every day there was some exciting news, and then finally peace was signed on Lünebury Heath.

Now the weather was sunny. Flags were out everywhere. We had two days of holiday. All over the country there were street parties. Neighbours, drawn together by fire-watching and war-time contacts, celebrated. Tables were put out in many Birmingham streets and children were given a festival tea with decorations. Taking old tins of food I went over to Hall Green and found long tables piled with delicacies not seen for years. Flags waved. The grown-ups waited on the children, and everyone was smiling.

Afterwards I went back to the red gaunt Regional Office, but none of the work there seemed of much consequence.

Gwendolen Freeman

Release

Soon after VE Day, before the war had ended in Asia, I had a great surprise. I received a note from an unknown editor. His paper was a small local bi-weekly that had hardly entered into my consciousness before. I had never even seen a copy.

The letter appealed for my help. I do not know how he had heard of me, but he said he understood that I was to return to the Daily later, but he needed only temporary assistance as his sub-editor was to leave the army in a few months. He had been editing the paper almost alone during the war and had been in great difficulties. He would be thankful if I could join him for a few months.

I should not have thought much of the appeal in my grand days, but I was grand no longer. The letter that I received one morning had an extraordinary effect on me. By midday when I sat at lunch at the rough tables of the canteen I was in a state of impatient delight. I could escape from this bondage. I could not bear it a moment longer. I looked at the queue of shabby red-faced men standing waiting for their food, heard the buzz of dull conversation and felt suddenly that I need be no longer of this world.

Work here in any case had sunk almost to nothing. The pressure of war-time service had finished. And I was wanted for real work somewhere else. It was like emerging from a tunnel.

I asked for my release, and those officers who had always been so personally kind said I might go. It all happened very quickly. They decided, justly, that I was not to be replaced. My secretary could be transferred to somebody else, and a lower official, the one who had long before talked to me about 'ear-oling', was to take charge of my monstrous collection of files – about twenty of them, I think, bulging in the filing cabinet. Heaven knows what was done with them in the end.

There was a small ceremony of farewell in Mr B.'s room on my last Saturday morning. Jokes were made about my criticisms of the ministry, and everybody laughed and shook hands. I discovered once more how kind and unaggressive these 'permanents' were, but it was embarrassing and I was left with a headache.

I stayed on clearing out my desk after everyone had gone, and all the time Swinburne's line:

168

'Blossom by blossom the spring begins'

was running in my head, set oddly to the tune of Lillibullero. Here was one more last time. I went down the dark steps into the windy street and could not quite believe my freedom. I was going out to the Hall Green family that afternoon. Gossip about children goes on when everything else changes.

Last Views

The following six months were a mixture of escape and trivialities. It took me a long time to be able to throw away even a scrap of paper without a feeling of guilt; to have a sense of being an individual again and not a cog in a machine; to express opinions without fearing I was breaking some rule. Meanwhile the world was in transition and I was awaiting my return to the Daily.

On the Monday after I left the Ministry of Labour I mounted rubber-smelling steps of a comparatively new building in the busy part of Corporation Street. The News's old offices had been bombed out, and it had taken a few rooms temporarily in this building. It had gathered what old furniture it could, and this was jammed together in one editorial room. We worked cheek by jowl in the haze of pipe and cigarette smoke, and it was not very comfortable. But I was content. I had been asked to come and there was plenty of work to do. A few weeks after I had arrived the editor went away on a holiday and left the whole paper to me.

In those months I had a view of Birmingham which might have been almost anywhere. All over the country papers were publishing – and still are – accounts of local crimes, anniversaries, scandals and funerals, making much of small events, giving a Police Court case earth-shaking importance. And, since people like to read about the things they know, and like to feel important, the small local papers have a solidity less known in most of the nationals. The News's rule was not to publish anything that had a national slant.

I sat at my shabby desk in the small News office putting together paragraphs culled from wedding forms that the paper sent out – what the bride, bridesmaids and mothers wore, who was best man, where the reception was held. If the family paid they could have a photograph

169

published, and the most lumpy brides and vacant-looking bridegrooms appeared on our pages. Much of the material generally came in from local people – on wispy paper, often written in sprawling longhand with spelling mistakes, often difficult to decipher. It all had to be cut and trimmed, and one might have thought that the stuff was not worth it, but it made Saturday reading for many simple people. The paper had been a godsend in the war for conveying news to men overseas. Afterwards I remember very little of it.

The atom bombs were dropped. VJ Day arrived – less sparkling than VE Day but still with a feeling of enormous relief. Autumn came, and I was still in the small cluttered room of the News. Then we heard that the sub-editor whom I was replacing would be out of the army by Christmas. The editor of the News went to the paper's owners and suggested that I should be kept on with the returning warrior, but they said they could not afford it. The editor wrote to me afterwards that he wished I could have stayed, as the assistant had moved to another paper almost at once.

I could not complain. I had been taken only to fill a gap. In any case change was going on everywhere, with people coming out of the Forces, war organisations shutting, workers returning home. Then I heard that L.P.H., editor of the Daily for so short a time, had died. Another of the leader writers had succeeded him.

This Mr H. had entertained me when I first came to Birmingham. Night after night he had sat in front of me as our office coach circled the suburbs. He was not a great favourite in the office because his temper was uncertain, but he once paid me a back-handed compliment. He told me one evening that he had met a friend who always read the women's page and enjoyed it. I was just beginning to thank him when he added, 'I told him I never read it myself.'

No. He was not very gracious, but I had known him a long time. In my eyes he had no aura as an editor. But he had the title. I wrote asking when I was to return. His answer surprised me. It was condescending and unfriendly. Once again I meditated that being elevated to a top job is not good for the character.

He said that no 'Women's Interests' page would be published again. I could come back to the Daily as a woman reporter, but he would not guarantee me more than six months. I heard later that he had treated men, due to return, in the same high-handed manner, and presently enquiries began as to why so many people who had been doing war jobs had not returned to the paper. Mr H. did not remain an editor for long.

But I was not to know this at the time. I reflected that Mr H. had stayed on in a cosy job while many people had lost everything in the war. But it was no good being angry. The old life had gone and many of the old faces. I did not answer Mr H.'s letter but looked for another job.

I had lived in Birmingham for fifteen years, and most of my friends were there. I had absorbed its history. Everything about it was familiar, even its telephone book. Like Geo. W. of long ago, I used to dislike London and feel that the Midlands were home. But now there was no work for me and I had to go.

I wrote to London papers and found work with a national weekly. Then everything went into reverse. I heard of two women who wanted my flat, and arranged for them to take it over with the furniture. In an atmosphere of unreality, not quite believing that I was going to leave the place, I said many goodbyes. And one Saturday afternoon before I left I crept back to the Daily office.

The watchman was as usual at the side entrance, but there was no-one else about. I walked warily down the warm, dim, silent passages. My old room was empty though with the faint smell of cigarette smoke. As of old I heard the ticking of the clock on the landing, the faint sound of machinery and nothing more.

The reproduction of the Leonardo cartoon that I had brought for my room when I arrived was still on the wall. I took it down. Working hastily, afraid of being discovered, I opened the door of my cupboard and found the pile of large account books and papers, which I had left four years before, still untouched. Hardly looking at the papers I dropped them into the waste-paper bin. But I left the account books. They might be needed for records.

There was still nobody about. Bearing my Leonardo I crept for the last time through the office which had once been home. Feeling like a ghost I slipped past the watchman and at last breathed free – free but with a sense of devastating loss.